Exploring the Word

Exploring the Word

100 Devotional Readings to Draw You Closer to God

VOLUME ONE

JOHN PHILLIPS

Exploring the Word: 100 Devotional Readings to Draw You Closer to God, Volume One

Previously published as *100 Devotions for Pastors and Church Leaders, Volume 1*

Published by Kregel Publications, a division of Kregel Inc., 2450 Oak Industrial Dr. NE, Grand Rapids, MI 49505.

Scripture taken from the King James Version. Italics added by the author.

ISBN 978-0-8254-4896-6

Printed in the United States of America

1 2 3 4 / 29 28 27 26 25 24

I dedicate this book to Betty, for whom these studies were written.

When I was courting her, Betty lived in California and I lived in North Carolina. Three thousand miles and three time zones stretched between us. As a result, much of our courting was done on the telephone. In time I ran out of things to say!

I decided to write her a devotional study every day. By the time I was finished I had written nearly three hundred devotions.

Here are one hundred of them, with her earnest desire that they might be as great a blessing to you as they have been to her.

CONTENTS

Devotion 1

It Was Good

Genesis 1–2

God is good—absolutely good. It is impossible for Him to do anything bad. The imprint of His goodness lies on all He does. It is evident, for instance, in every step and every stage of the work of creation as recorded in Genesis 1–2.

Out there in space, the vast machinery of the universe pulsated and roared, swirling around the great white throne of God. Countless billions of stars and their satellites were hurrying through intangible space on prodigious orbits at inconceivable velocities and with mathematical precision. God made it all, and it was all good. The angels of God around His throne shouted and sang in awe and wonder at this display of omniscient wisdom and omnipotent power.

Somewhere, in the midst of this sublime activity, there swirled a galaxy of some 100 billion stars, a galaxy we call the Milky Way. One of those stars was unique; we call it the Sun. It had gathered around it a solar system of planets. One of those planets we call Earth.

For some reason, barely hinted at in Scripture, this planet was "without form, and void," and darkness concealed the face of the deep. It was about to become the platform, however, on which God would stage a demonstration of the fact that He was good as well as great.

"Light be!" He said. And instantly light was. Just like that! Light reigned. And it was good as God is good. The light revealed a chaos of tossing water, a vast and shoreless sea. No land raised its head above the heaving waves and smothering mist. God called for an atmosphere to be formed. At once, two vast oceans appeared, one above and one below, with a far-flung firmament between, a space for clouds to congregate, a playground for weather to have its way. God said that it was good.

But still the rolling seas held restless empire over all the world. God put an instant end to that. The continents arose, towering peaks appeared, and the land threw off the mantle of the sea. And it was good.

Then God brought forth life in countless varieties and forms. The seas swarmed with life. The sky was taken over by birds and other winged creatures. Vegetation threw a garment of green over vast segments of the earth. Forests sprang up everywhere. Creatures great and small grazed the glens and roamed the vast forests of a pristine world. And it was good.

Then God made man, made him in His own image and after His own likeness, made him to be inhabited by God Himself. He was to be a creature apart, able to think and feel and decide, able to speak and sing, able to appreciate beauty, control his environment, rule the world, and worship God. And it was good. Everything was good. In fact, it was very good. God said so. And so it was. The word the Holy Spirit uses for "good" means "beautiful." The Holy Spirit used it seven times in telling us the tale.

And then God said, *"It is not good!"* For though Adam was monarch of all he surveyed, though all things were under his feet, though he was indwelt by God, and though he loved God and obeyed God and had daily fellowship with God, he ruled his vast empire alone. The birds of the air had companions to share their nests. The foxes had mates to share their dens. Only Adam roamed the world alone. It was not good.

So God went to work again. One day Adam awoke from a deep sleep, and what he saw must have made him think he was still asleep or in a dream! For there she stood, his counterpart, the woman God had especially made for him. And suddenly everything was good. God is good—that was what it all said. Far-flung galaxies, creatures from the seas and skies, all of nature has one song to sing:

How good is the God we adore,
Our faithful unchangeable Friend,
Whose love is as great as His power,
And knows neither measure nor end.[1]

---

1. Joseph Hart, "How Good Is the God We Adore," 1759.

Devotion 2

The Lesser Light

Genesis 1:16

The moon is about one quarter the size of the earth. It orbits the earth at a mean distance of 238,866 miles and at an average speed of 2,287 miles an hour. It takes the moon a little over twenty-seven days to complete one orbit of the earth. Its temperature can vary from 260°F in the sun to -280°F in the shade. The moon has fascinated mankind from the dawn of time. People in their ignorance have worshiped it. Abraham, before he met the true and living God, dwelt at Ur, a center of moon worship in his day. Possibly he once worshiped it himself.

The moon was doubtless created "in the beginning" when God created the heaven and the earth. According to the Genesis creation narrative, the moon was appointed to function on the fourth day of creation. It is from the movement of the sun that we get our concept of the year and the day; it is from the movement of the moon that we get our concept of the month.

The moon is of interest to us theologically. It can be viewed, for instance, as a type of the church. Consider, first, the origin of the moon, a matter that has been the subject of considerable debate. One view is that it was spun off from the surface of the earth and that the vast cavity, now filled by the Pacific Ocean, was one result of this. If that is so, then the moon was once part of this world but is now seated on high in the heavens and, as such, gives us a picture of believers who comprise the church. The church is made up of people who once belonged to Earth but are now seated with Christ in heavenly places, far above the restless world that wars below.

The function of the moon is to rule the night. It is seated on high to cast light upon the earth during the period when the sun is absent. It has no light of its own. The only way the moon can shine is by reflecting the light of the sun; but even at that, it can reflect only 7 percent of the light that strikes its surface. In astronomical terms, the magnitude (i.e., the scale of brightness) of the full moon is very small. By contrast, the brightness of the sun's light is more than 400,000 times as great as that of the moon.

Similarly, the function of the church is to shed light upon the earth during the dark period covered by the absence of Christ. The light the church spreads is very dim, however, as compared with the light of Christ. But pale as it is by comparison with the light of Christ, the light believers bring to bear on human affairs is better than nothing at all. The church does not generate light; for, like the moon, it has no light of its own. It reflects the light of Christ. That in itself is a most important role.

The moon waxes and wanes, all the way from a full, bright disk down to a small crescent and even into darkness itself. Moreover, it can be eclipsed. This happens when the earth comes between the moon and the sun. In like manner, there are times in the history of the church when revival comes and the church shines very brightly indeed. The world benefits greatly from its light at such times. There are other times, however, when the testimony of the church grows dim and darkness reigns. Tragically, too, there are times of apostasy when the church succumbs to the philosophies and errors of the world, and its light is eclipsed.

Then, too, the moon exercises power over the seas by causing the tides. Every day it pulls the waters of the oceans up along the shore lands and into the mouths of rivers. The seas are powerless, great as they are, to resist the tremendous influence of the moon, though it seems so remote and far away. In the typology of Scripture, the *seas* represent the troubled, storm-tossed nations of the world, just as the *earth* represents the nation of Israel. The moon reminds us of the enormous influence the church has had throughout history over the affairs of humanity. People discount the influence of the church, but that does not change the fact. The prayers of God's people and the preaching of its ambassadors in the power of the Spirit has its effect on every shore.

Devotion 3

The Temptation of Eve

Genesis 3:1–6

He is called "the old serpent." Three chapters in from the beginning of the Bible we see him for the first time; three chapters in from the end of the Bible we see him for the last time. He came into the garden of Eden to effect the fall and ruin of the human race. He will end up in the eternal flames of the lake of fire.

His first goal in the garden was to disarm Eve by robbing her of the only weapon she had, the Word of God. The Bible Eve had was small enough—just two brief verses—but it was enough. Sadly, she misquoted it three times. Twice she subtracted from what God had actually said, and once she added to it. After that she was in Satan's power. Satan based his attack on a *doubt,* a *denial,* and a *delusion,* and swiftly carried the day.

"Yea, hath God said?" That was the *doubt.* "How do you know God said that? You only have it by transmission from Adam. You weren't there when this 'Word' was given. How can you prove it is the Word of God? How do you know it is true?"

"Ye shall not surely die." That was the *denial.* "How ridiculous! Death for eating fruit from a tree! What nonsense! Besides, God is a loving God. Can you seriously believe that God would put you to death just for taking a bite from a piece of fruit? Death? There is nothing to fear about death. Death is the greatest adventure of all. God just wants to frighten you. In any case, you won't die. You'll begin to live."

"Ye shall be as gods." That was the *delusion.* It was the promise of freedom from narrowness and from unacceptable restrictions on one's behavior. It promised access to a wonderful, glorious world of knowledge. Life in a new dimension could be hers. She could become a liberated woman.

Inherent in the temptation was an appeal to "the lust of the eyes," because the tree was "pleasant to the eyes." There was an appeal to "the lust of the flesh," because the tree was "good for food." There was an appeal to "the pride of life," because it was "to be desired to make one wise." This threefold appeal promised access to mysterious and marvelous hidden secrets. Adam and Eve would become like God Himself. The Serpent's wiles were successful. In fact, he has not had to change his approach throughout all the course of human history. All temptation rises from these three primeval appeals.

Once Eve had accepted the Devil's lie and rejected God's truth, the rest followed as a matter of course. Satan led Eve from one foolish act to another, each downward step preparing the way for the next one.

First, she "saw." The Serpent fastened Eve's gaze upon the desired object. Soon she could not take her eyes off it. A large percentage of temptation comes to us through our eyes. Satan's plan was to turn *the look into a lust.*

Next, she "took." Now the plan was to turn the *desire into a deed*. That had to be Eve's decision. Satan can *persuade* but he cannot *push*. He could suggest to the Lord, for instance, that He throw Himself down from the temple pinnacle; but he could not push Him down.

Then, she "did eat." Now the plan was to turn *the choice into a chain.* Jesus said, "Whosoever committeth sin is the servant of sin" (John 8:34). Habits grow. They are flimsy enough at first, but each time we repeat the deed, the power of the habit is increased, until the habit itself takes over the will and we find ourselves in chains.

Finally, she "gave." That was the ultimate goal. The *sinner* became a *seducer.* It is significant that the Serpent did not tempt Adam; Eve did.

Thus sin entered the world and death by sin (Rom. 5:12). The fall was complete. Satan had won. Death reigned. Satan had won? Not forever! For Jesus came, and the Serpent was no match for Him. His little bag of tricks was scorned by Christ. Satan lost, and now he lives in terror of the return from heaven of the victorious Christ. And well he should.

Devotion 4

By Faith Enoch Was Translated

Genesis 5:21–24; Hebrews 11:5; Jude 14–15

"There were giants in the earth in those days," God says (Gen. 6:4). They appeared in the godless line of Cain. They were prodigies of strength, knowledge, and wickedness. But there were other giants, too, unheralded and unsung, mighty men of God, giants of the faith. There were men like Seth, the founder of the godly line; men like Noah and Enoch who spoke to contemporary issues, warning of judgment to come; and Abel, noble martyr of the faith. The first man to leave this earth was Abel. He died, both murdered and martyred, hero and saint. The second man was Enoch—caught up boldly into heaven by way of the rapture. A giant indeed! Our thoughts here are taken up with Enoch.

We think first of *his times.* They overlapped with the days of Noah and displayed the same hallmark. It was a time of great *mental activity.* Cain, a vagabond of a man, surprisingly enough conceived the idea of gathering an ever-growing world population into cities. Rural lifestyles with their innate conservation gave way to urban living. Great cities attract talent and breed crime. It was so in Enoch's day. All fields of human endeavor experienced tremendous innovations and growth. Science, engineering, and technology took gigantic strides and produced the skills needed to build the ark. Art expressed itself in musical entertainment and metal-working. It was God who enabled them to achieve these things and to fill their houses with good things. Their response was to tell God to be gone. What could the Almighty do for them that they could not do for themselves (Job 22:16–18)?

So it was not only a time of mental activity but was also a time of *material prosperity.* They were eating and drinking and marrying and giving in marriage, all legitimate things but things that were blighted by their unbelief.

Moreover it was a time of *moral depravity.* "The earth . . . was corrupt," the Holy Spirit declared (Gen. 6:11). People employed their imaginative powers to devise wicked pleasures and pastimes. Their every thought was evil. They lived to gratify their lusts and to pursue perversion with the blessing of all.

Finally it was an age of *monumental apostasy.* The godly line dwindled to the sum of one man's family. The Cainites abandoned all pretense of religion. Of the dozen names in the line of Cain listed in the record, only two had any reference to God (Mehujael and Methusael). In contrast, those recorded in the godly line often have annotations alongside their names, comments that help us see how godliness was kept alive on the earth despite the increasing wickedness of the Cainites and the dwindling numbers of the Sethites.

The godlessness of the Cainites brought in the final apostasy. Occultism flourished and gave rise to a "New Age" movement. People began to explore the deep things of Satan and to delve into forbidden secrets. Because their forebearers ate fruit from a fatal tree of knowledge, the Cainites' eyes were opened. They became as gods and plunged into the ultimate evil. A strange hybrid progeny appeared, and wickedness inundated the earth.

We think next of Enoch's *testimony.* Enoch was the heir of the ages, descendant of a long line of patriarchs of the faith. The torch of testimony was handed on to him by his forebears, and he raised it high for three hundred years before handing it on to his son. As apostasy increased, so Enoch preached the more boldly. He warned of the coming of the Lord in judgment (Jude 14–15). He foresaw a coming holocaust of wrath. He denounced ungodliness. He set a date for the day of doom. He called his son by the significant name "Methuselah," meaning "when he dies, it shall come." Not even such anointed preaching as Enoch's, however, could stem the tide. Wickedness was in the saddle, riding high, wide and handsome across the face of the world. Nothing could stop it but judgment.

Finally, we have *his translation.* For Enoch did not die. He was carried bodily into heaven. The rapture came, and he was gone, caught away in a moment, in the twinkling of an eye, from family and friends, from business partners and fellow saints. A voice for God was suddenly stilled on the earth. The ungodly took it in their stride, doubtless glad that he was gone. It would save them the trouble of killing him. A silence fell, an ominous silence, not broken until the voice of Noah rang out, and the judgment, long promised, finally fell. Thus Enoch was a candidate for rapture. So are we who love the Lord.

Devotion 5

Mount Moriah

Genesis 22

Sir Edmund Hillary reached the summit of Mount Everest on May 29, 1953. At 29,028 feet above sea level, he stood at the top of the world, thanks to teamwork, good equipment, and cooperating weather. But Everest is dwarfed by Mount Moriah just as Mount Moriah is dwarfed by Mount Calvary. Mount Moriah, after all, represents only one of the pictorial shadows cast by Calvary. But even the shadow has a great deal to say.

We think, first, of *the supreme test.* The story begins and ends with the same words: "And it came to pass after these things" (22:1). For Calvary was the *consummation* of a plan, thought out in eternity, to bring salvation to mankind. Many things led up to the death of Christ on that cruel Roman cross on that skull-shaped hill in that ancient city of Jerusalem, famous for stoning its saints and slaughtering its seers.

"And it came to pass after these things" (22:20). For Calvary was the *commencement* of a plan, thought out in eternity, to bring into being a church. The story of Mount Moriah in Genesis 22 prepares us for the call of Rebekah in Genesis 24 just as the mystery of the cross prepares us for the mystery of the church. All was foreseen by Jehovah, but Abraham did not yet know that.

Out of the blue came the terrible test: "Take now thy son, thine only son Isaac, whom thou lovest, and get thee into the land of Moriah; and offer him there." All Abraham's love, all his hopes, all the future of his race rested in Isaac. And all his joy and laughter and all of his plans and purposes were centered in his son. Must it all end abruptly in blood and flame? What a test!

We think not only of the supreme test but also of *the supreme trust.* Abraham had God's word for it: "*In Isaac* shall thy seed be called" (Gen. 21:12). Would his trust reach beyond the tomb and the death of all his hopes? Hebrews 11:19 says that it did. For Abraham dared to believe that if he offered up Isaac, God would raise him back to life. That was sublime faith that enabled him to say to his servants: "Abide ye here . . . and I and the lad will go yonder and worship, *and come again* to you" (Gen. 22:5).

So the wood, a burden borne by others up to now was thrust upon Isaac. More! Isaac could see the knife (speaking of death), and the fire (speaking of that which comes after death). Yet in perfect love, obedience, and confidence in his father, he went with him to the dreaded mount. "Both of them together." "Both of them together." The Holy Spirit writes it down twice (Gen. 22:6, 8). Isaac was not dragged fighting and protesting to the hill of death. As with Christ, who went willingly to Calvary, so with Isaac. He and his father were in this thing together.

Which brings us to *the supreme truth.* The whole story is obviously a type. *A lamb would be provided.* That is the supreme truth this story tells. God said, in effect, to Abraham: "I want you as a human father to take your only begotten son to a place called Mount Moriah, a place foreseen by Me, and I want you to offer him up there as a burnt offering so that the world may know what it will cost Me, as a heavenly Father, to take My only begotten Son to a place called Mount Calvary and offer Him up there as an atonement for all mankind." For that, too, was "foreseen by Jehovah." More! It was foreseen by Jehovah that there would be no ram caught by its horns to spare God's own dear Son when His time came. As Abraham watched the flames ascend, to consume the sacrifice God had provided, how he would have appreciated the words of this great hymn of the church:

> When I think that God, His Son not sparing,
> Sent Him to die, I scarce can take it in,
> That on the cross, my burden gladly bearing,
> He bled and died to take away my sin.[1]

---

1. Carl Boberg, "How Great Thou Art," 1885.

Devotion 6

Wilt Thou Go with This Man?

Genesis 24

The story of Abraham sending his servant to find a bride for Isaac is a full-length Old Testament portrait of Christ and His church.

All the initiative was with Abraham (who stands for the Father). The servant, sent forth into the world to seek the needed bride, represents the Holy Spirit. Isaac, seated with his father, pictures the Lord Jesus.

The servant did not go abroad to speak about himself but only to magnify the father and the son. When he found the prospective bride, he used no coercion. He simply presented the facts and extended an invitation.

He did, however, come bearing gifts. And here the difference between Rebekah and her brother, Laban, is seen. When Laban saw the earrings and the bracelets on his sister, he was all ears and eyes. He wanted such gifts, the spectacular gifts that accredited the servant and proved his mission to be valid. He reminds us of Simon Magus, who wanted to acquire an apostolic gift for his own enrichment and aggrandizement. It nearly cost him his soul (Acts 8:9–25). Rebekah, by contrast, received the gifts but soon lost interest in them. Her thoughts were not on the gifts but on the groom.

And so the great question was asked: "Wilt thou go with this man?" (Gen. 24:58). "I will," was her simple reply. The story now focuses on the servant and the bride-to-be. There are four steps in the story.

First, we see *Rebekah leaving*, for there had to be a complete break with the past. All that belonged to her past life became a fading memory. Her thoughts were on the future for she knew that, when her traveling days were done, one would be awaiting her arrival at his home. Where he was, there she would be also. She had never seen him, but she believed in him. The unnamed servant had done his work well. She had the gifts, also, to remind her of the one who was awaiting her.

Next, we see *Rebekah learning.* The unknown servant (type of the Holy Spirit) was now her comforter and her guide. It was not left up to her to find her way to Isaac and his father's house. It was the responsibility of the servant to bring her safely home. She must have had a thousand questions. He would delight in telling her more and more about the one she had set out to meet. He would tell her of Isaac's miraculous birth and how he was the father's well-beloved and "only begotten" son. He would tell how Isaac had become obedient unto death and how he had came back, as it were, from the dead.

Then we see *Rebekah longing.* Time passed, and Rebekah's thoughts dwelt less and less on her old life. More and more she focused on the new life she had chosen and on the joy that was set before her. Isaac was both the center and the circumference of her thoughts. The more the servant told her of the father's well-beloved, the more he became increasingly real to her. The more she learned of him, the more she longed for him. And, although she had not seen him, love for him took root in her heart.

Finally, we see *Rebekah looking.* As the journey reached its close, the servant began to prepare her increasingly for the longed-for meeting soon to come. "He will be coming for you," he would say. "It could be any day now. The time of watching and waiting will be over soon." Rebekah would pay more attention to herself, to preparing herself, so that she would be ready when Isaac came and not be ashamed at his coming. Then one day he came.

And a new chapter in the story of redemption was begun.

Devotion 7

When God Makes a Move

Exodus

It was time for a change. It might have seemed to some to be long overdue. Not so! God moves according to His own timetable. He had long before told Abraham that his seed would be in a foreign land for four hundred years. The date for the change had been marked on God's calendar all the time. Now the time had come. The children of Israel, enslaved in Egyptian bondage, were to be redeemed, removed, and resettled. It is instructive to observe four spiritual laws that seem to come into effect at such times.

First, there were *changing times.* The Israelite presence in Goshen had long troubled the Egyptians in a general sort of a way. They were different. They belonged to a different God. What if they should side one day with one of Egypt's foes? Then there arose that king who "knew not Joseph" (Exod. 1:8). And all of a sudden everything was changed. The comfortable state of compromise was over. It was the first step in a movement that would change the world.

Now came *churning tides.* The Israelites awoke one morning to the din of war. Pharaoh's army had marched into Goshen. Behind them came the barbed wire, the guard dogs trained to kill, the chains, the taskmasters, and all the paraphernalia of oppression, and a new, terrible law: "Cast all newborn males into the Nile." Churning tides, indeed. The people of God had become too comfortable in this present evil world. They must be made to see it as God sees it, as the sworn enemy of God and all things holy. Oppression and more oppression would come, for now the world's mask was off, and its hideous, hate-marked face revealed. It is God's way to use the churning tides for His own ends.

What churning tides were unleashed in 1939, for instance, when the German army stormed into Poland. The turmoil went on and on until the whole world was engulfed. Millions of people were uprooted from their homes and sent to distant lands. Out of it came a new generation of men and women, who had traveled to those lands and who went back as missionaries. The churning tides prepared the way. The modern missionary era began.

Next came *cheerless toils.* In Egypt the people of God were put to a new kind of work. They made bricks for Pharaoh. Pharaoh had vast plans. He wanted treasure cities built. He wanted bricks. The hated Hebrews were whipped into line. They must make his bricks. More and more bricks. He urged on his slave drivers, and they goaded the unhappy Hebrews. They must have wondered, "Was this the way to the Promised Land?" It seemed like a cynical joke.

And then the unexpected and unexplained took place. The people began to multiply. The more pressure the world applied, the more the people of God multiplied. It was the same in the book of Acts with the infant church. The pressure of persecution went on for about three hundred years until there were more Christians than pagans in Rome. Yes! God was still on the throne!

Finally we see certain *chosen tools.* There was Jochabed and Amram, who dared to have a son in such troubled and terrible times. There was Moses, the child born to become a kinsman-redeemer to Israel in the fullness of time. There was Miriam, the brave sister of Moses who watched over the infant in his ark of rushes in the Nile, fearless of Egyptian soldiers and Nile crocodiles alike. Others followed. There was Aaron, sent to be a companion to Moses and high priest to Israel, and Joshua, chosen of Moses to succeed him and to take possession at last of the long-promised land. Though in the onward march of time God buries His workers, He still carries on His work. We'll understand it better by and by.

Devotion 8

Jochabed

Exodus 2:1–9

Jochabed was a Levite. So was her husband. In those days the Levites had not yet been elevated to the priestly rank, but they must have had some bent toward God, not evident in other tribes. Perhaps they were the ones who kept alive the stories and truths now written down in the book of Genesis. In any case, the Holy Spirit deems it important enough to note the fact that Amram and Jochabed were Levites.

Jochabed was the mother of Moses. The first significant fact was that *she had him.* It seems to have been a deliberate decision. She and her husband, we are told, were "not afraid of the king's commandment" (Heb. 11:23). The death sentence had already been signed into law—all Hebrew male children were to be thrown into the Nile. (No wonder, later on, Moses turned the water of the Nile into blood.) So, down there in that ghetto in Goshen, Jochabed gave birth to a baby boy who would one day humble Egypt in the dust and change the course of history forever.

Then *she hid him.* The boy was born under the sentence of death. She was determined to see him soundly saved. So she began by hiding him from the world and its prince by hiding him *in the haven of her home.* She firmly shut the door of her house and kept out all the evil influences of the world. A godly home was her first line of defense against the world and its ways. God intends that our homes should be sanctuaries against the world and everything for which it stands. The world has its *prince,* motivated by a malice against the human race that defies description. The world has its *programs,* and they are diametrically opposed to the Word of God. The world has its *pleasures,* but the Bible calls them "the pleasures of sin" (Heb. 11:25). Jochabed made sure that all such things were firmly shut out of her home.

But the time came, as it always does, when Moses could no longer be hidden at home. At this point, Jochabed exercised faith. She said, "How does God save those who are under the sentence of death?" She thought about Noah and his ark, and then she made a little ark for Moses. She put him in the ark and put the ark in the river. Now it was all up to God. All she could do now was watch and pray. She had now hidden him in *the hollow of God's hand.*

Finally, *she held him.* A series of events took place in which God demonstrated His sovereignty and His ability to defy the prince of this world. As a result Moses was adopted into the Egyptian royal family, but not until Jochabed was given the opportunity of nurturing him. Evidently she devoted her time to teaching Moses the truths that he later immortalized in the book of Genesis. Especially she drilled him in the story of Joseph (one quarter of Genesis is devoted to Joseph), the story of a young man who had lived victoriously for God in the courts of Pharaoh.

Jochabed held him! No Egyptian school, no Egyptian seduction, no Egyptian sophistication had a chance. Jochabed had done her work well. She had wedded her boy to God's Word, and God's Word held him against all the world could offer. What a woman! Such women are desperately needed today.

Devotion 9

Moses at Horeb

Exodus 3:1; 17:6; 33:6

Horeb is mentioned three times in Exodus in connection with Moses. Horeb and Sinai are closely linked. Horeb was the mountain range; Sinai was one of its peaks. It was at Horeb Moses met God.

The first time it was at the burning bush. God showed His *government,* His absolute sovereignty over human affairs. Moses came, with his father-in-law's flocks, to what the Holy Spirit describes as "the backside of the desert" (Exod. 3:1). It is also called "the mountain of God." That is significant. When a person is in the will of God, everything about him bears the mark of God—a man becomes "a man of God," a rod becomes "the rod of God," a word becomes "the word of God," a mountain becomes "the mountain of God."

So Moses came to Horeb and to the burning bush. He was drawn aside to see this most unusual of usual sights—a bush ablaze with fierce flames and wrapped in fire. Yet, despite the devouring fire, the bush was not consumed. Moses was arrested. However, God had to get beyond the eye of Moses to his ear, for "faith cometh by hearing" the Bible says (Rom. 10:17). "Moses! Moses! Remove your shoes," God said. "And Moses hid his face," the Holy Spirit adds (Exod. 3:6).

A thornbush in the fire but not consumed. That thornbush was Israel, and the fire was the growing oppression of the pharaoh. Yet, for all his power, Pharaoh could not make an end of God's people. And who was this Pharaoh? A speck of dust, inflated with pride, surrounded by meaningless pomp, worshiping cats and cows and crocodiles and creeping things.

God began with Moses' feet. He told him to remove the shoes from off his feet. That is where He usually begins. Our feet have to do with our standing. When the stone came hurtling out of eternity to smash Nebuchadnezzar's golden image, it did not strike the head. It smote the feet. So, at Horeb, there was a lesson in *government.* True, the bush was ablaze; but God was in the bush, and that changed everything. Pharaoh was up against God.

The second time Horeb is mentioned, Moses gets a lesson in *grace.* At the beginning of any new venture, God allows us to be tested. Thus Israel came to Rephidim and the shadow of a great fear. For there was no water, no water at all, not even bitter water as at Marah. Cattle lowed in anguish. Children cried to their parents. The people turned on Moses and threatened to kill him. Moses turned to God: "They be almost ready to stone me," he cried (Exod. 17:4). "Take your rod," God commanded. It was a rod of judgment. With that rod Moses had turned the rivers of Egypt to blood. It was poised to fall on this rebellious people. Instead, it fell on the rock—and the water of life poured forth. It was a lesson in grace, the rock being a type of Christ.

The third time Horeb is mentioned, Moses gets a lesson in *glory.* He had been summoned by God back up the mount, and he had been gone a long time, or so it seemed to rebellious Israel. Apostasy took over. Aaron made a golden calf, and the people abandoned themselves to lustful singing and lewd dancing. Then Moses returned, and judgment followed. In despair Moses threw himself into the arms of God. "[Show] me now thy way," he said (Exod. 33:13), and then, more daring still, "[show] me thy glory" (v. 18). And so God hid this troubled servant in the cleft of the rock, for only in such a secure hiding place could he be safe when God's effulgent glory was revealed. God showed Moses His goodness and His grace—for that is His glory, as we shall know at last in glory itself.

Devotion 10

The Gods of Egypt

Exodus 12:12

The Egyptian civilization was unrivaled in the ancient world. Its artifacts fill our museums and draw countless crowds who come to wonder and to stare. The Egyptians had eaten well of the tree of knowledge. *Their brilliant minds were enlightened.* We read of Moses that he was "learned in all the wisdom of the Egyptians" (Acts 7:22). His knowledge was coextensive with that of the learned doctors at whose feet he sat. The Egyptians excelled in the arts and sciences. They had the technology and industry to build the pyramids. They were marvelous engineers. They were experts in agriculture, in navigation, in warfare, and in astronomy. They built monuments that became wonders of the world and have withstood the test of time.

To this day we marvel at the pyramids. From a distance they look like mountains, rising sharply against the sky. Everything about them is big. Some 2.5 million blocks of limestone, weighing from two to five tons apiece (an aggregate of some 6 million tons), make up the mass of the Great Pyramid alone. When Moses and the enslaved Hebrews saw them, they were already at least a thousand years old. How did the Egyptians build such things? We still do not know. We only know their brilliant minds were enlightened. Moses was called to wage a one-man war against this brilliant people.

But there was another side to the Egyptians. *Their foolish hearts were darkened.* "Professing themselves to be wise, they became fools, and changed the glory of the uncorruptible God into an image" (Rom. 1:22–23). Egypt was crowded with graven images, and their pantheon teemed with gods. There was *Hathor,* the sky goddess, sometimes depicted as a cow. There was *Osiris,* who was married to his sister, *Isis.* There was *Set,* the jealous and murderous brother of *Osiris.* There was *Thoth,* the moon god, the recorder of the deeds of the dead. There was the jackal-headed *Anubis,* the despoiler. And many more. It was against these gods of Egypt, led by Pharaoh himself, the incarnation of *Ra,* the sun god, that Moses was sent. And it was these false and foolish gods Moses was to expose as empty, shattered, and defeated in his hand-to-hand combat with Pharaoh.

The gods of Egypt were *prevalent.* Every phase of Egyptian life was governed by the gods. They dominated life from the womb to the tomb. Moreover, they were *preposterous,* usually depicted as humans with the heads and features of animals and birds. There was the lion-headed *Sekhmet,* a goddess sent to punish people if they neglected the gods. There was *Anubis,* with the head of a jackal. There was no end to it, cats and crocodiles, bats and beetles. And the folly of it all lay in the fact that these gods were not only false, but they were also *powerless.*

It was God's avowed intent, right from the start, to expose the utter impotence of these gods (Exod. 12:12). Aaron's rod turned into a serpent and swallowed the rods of the magicians and poked fun at the serpent image Pharaoh wore as a crown on his brow. The Nile was worshiped as a source of life, so it was turned to blood. Frogs were worshiped as a symbol of fruitfulness, so God used them to plague the Egyptians. The pestilence on the cattle was aimed at the worship of animals. The plague of darkness showed *Ra,* the sun god, to be powerless. And, of course, the last, terrible plague that brought death to every home exposed the impotence of each and every Egyptian god.

So there Pharaoh sat, in all his pomp and splendor, with the resources of an empire at his command, powerless. And there stood Moses, the despised and detested shepherd, an abomination to the Egyptians, in his homespun, peasant's robes, clothed with power from on high. On the one hand, Egypt's ludicrous gods; on the other hand, Israel's living God. It is still that way. Forty years before, Moses had decided whose side he was on. Adopted into the Egyptian royal family, educated in Egypt's finest schools, offered pleasure and power and boundless prosperity and the very throne itself, it would seem, Moses chose the living God, not this world's tin and tinsel gods. We must do the same.

Devotion II

The Ashes and the Fire

Leviticus 1–7

The first seven chapters of Leviticus are concerned with the various offerings the Hebrew people were to bring to God. The details were given meticulously, and more and more requirements were added. We tend to read these chapters with varying degrees of bewilderment and impatience, for all these ritual requirements belong to the long, long ago. Why should we be concerned with them now? They are obsolete. Calvary and Pentecost have swept them away. Besides, the meaning of all these things escapes us. Even the Jews themselves would be hard put to interpret the true meaning of all these rituals and rules.

Maybe so. But they are evidently of great interest to God. He inspired the writing down of all these details. These verses are as much "God-breathed" as our favorite New Testament texts. Indeed, God was not content with writing it all down once—burnt offering, meal offering, peace offering, sin offering, trespass offering. When He had finished, He went back over the same ground, adding fresh details in the form of sundry "laws"—the *law* of the burnt offering, the *law* of the sin offering, and so on. He delights in every detail for, one and all, the offerings speak of Christ in His flawless life and atoning death.

The *law* of the burnt offering was concerned with two added details, with the fire and with the ashes. The *fire* was to never go out. That reminds us that God's wrath against sin is as fierce today as it was when it kindled the lake of fire. The crime of Calvary has heated it seven times hotter than before. It will never go out. That is a terrible truth, but it is consistent with the holiness of God.

The *law* of the burnt offering was concerned also with the *ashes.* They were infinitely precious to God. After the fire had burned all night, consuming the burnt offering, the priest approached the brazen altar in fine linen. Reverently he collected the ashes and carried them outside the camp to a clean place.

The ashes remind us of a great truth. We can stir a smoldering fire and get sparks and blow upon the embers and bring back the fire and, with fresh fuel, again have roaring flames. But we can stir ashes forever and get nothing. There is nothing left to burn. This tells us that it is impossible to stir God's wrath against the believer. The sacrificial work of Christ is so complete, His substitutionary work so effective, that nothing can ever rekindle God's wrath so far as we are concerned. That is consistent with the love of God. Neither His *eternal* wrath nor His *end-time* wrath can fall upon us. He has *not* appointed *us* to wrath but to obtain salvation (I Thess. 5:9).

Years ago a fire was sweeping across the prairie, driven by the wind. A man and his family stood in its path. The man kindled a fire at his feet. It took hold and, driven by the wind, burned out a swath of the grass. "Come and stand where the fire has been," the man said. The family did so, and the approaching holocaust passed them by. There was nothing left there to burn.

That is where the believer stands—where the fire has been. His salvation is assured.

Devotion 12

The Leper

Leviticus 14

Leprosy! Oh, the horror of it! It was a doom worse than death. For a while a leper could hide his disease and pretend to be well, but the disease would spread. Worse still, it could be caught by others. And there was no cure. All that could be done was to put the leper outside the camp and make him cover his upper lip and cry "unclean" if anyone came that way. There is a notable difference made between sickness and leprosy in the Bible. Jesus *healed* the sick, but He *cleansed* lepers. The Hebrews regarded leprosy as "the stroke of God." There was no hope for the leper. He was unclean and excommunicated and could look forward only to death.

Five Old Testament lepers come to mind. Astonishingly enough, the first leper in Scripture was *Moses* (Exod. 4:6–7)! His leprosy was intended to *reveal* to him that he was no better than Pharaoh. The only difference was that he had accepted God's grace and Pharaoh had not. Before Moses could pronounce judgment on Pharaoh, he had to pronounce judgment on himself. Hand and heart he was a leper in God's sight.

Equally astonishing, the second leper was *Miriam,* the honored sister of Moses (Num. 12). Her leprosy was a *rebuke.* She had criticized Moses for marrying an Ethiopian woman, so God smote her. It is a serious thing to speak slightingly of God's servants. Thanks to the intercession of Moses, Miriam was healed.

The next leper was *Naaman* (2 Kings 5). In this case, God intended to *restore.* Jesus reminded the people of Nazareth that there were many lepers in Israel in the days of Elisha. "None of them was cleansed, saving Naaman the Syrian," He said. The people of Nazareth were so enraged at Jesus for speaking these words that they tried to murder Him (Luke 4:27–29). The cleansing of Naaman illustrates God's way of salvation.

All Naaman's preconceived ideas as to how he would be saved had to be set aside. He had to go to the place appointed by God. He had to accept God's terms, humble his pride, and receive salvation as a gift. So do we.

The next leper was *Gehazi* (2 Kings 5). Here the leprosy was intended to *repay*. Elisha had gone to great lengths to teach Naaman that salvation could not be purchased. Gehazi ruined it all by running after the departing Naaman and asking for money and merchandise in Elisha's name. The prophet's swift judgment was terrible. He smote Gehazi with Naaman's leprosy.

Then came *King Uzziah* (2 Chron. 26). This leprosy was intended to *restrain* Uzziah when, swollen with pride and presumption, he tried to intrude into the priests' office, knowing full well that the Law separated between "church" and state. God smote him right there in the temple, and he remained a leper to the day of his death.

The Levitical code made provision for the cleansing of the leper. Probably, however, the only time it was ever used, throughout the entire Old Testament period, was in the case of Miriam.

The cleansing (Lev. 14) revolved around three focal points. First, there was the leper's *remarkable condition*. Apart from Moses, Miriam, and Naaman, we read of no other leper being cured in Old Testament times. So, it would indeed have been a remarkable thing had one showed up at the house of the nearest priest to announce himself restored—just the very thing Jesus invariably told lepers He cleansed to go and do (see Matt. 8:1–4).

Next, was the leper's *ritual cleansing*. Once satisfied that the leprosy was gone, the priest took two birds. One of these he killed in an earthen vessel over running water. This pointed to the *redemptive* work of Christ. The earthen vessel spoke of the Lord's body, which was the instrument whereby He suffered death. The running water symbolized the Holy Spirit for it was "through the eternal Spirit [He] offered himself without spot to God" (Heb. 9:14). The other bird was dipped in the blood of the first one. The leper was pronounced clean, and the living bird was released to carry the testifying blood up to heaven—pointing to the *resurrection* and ascension work of Christ.

Finally, we have the leper's *restored communion*. This took more time and called for a much deeper appreciation of Calvary than that symbolized by the two birds. The cleansed leper was finally allowed back into the camp, but fellowship was not immediately restored. He had to "tarry abroad" (i.e., live out of doors) for seven days. After further ritual cleansing, he was pronounced clean. But then came a most elaborate ritual involving a trespass offering, a sin offering, and a burnt offering and the application of the blood (the finished work of Christ) and of the oil (the continuing work of the Spirit) to his extremities. In all this, the priest was prominent (pointing to the unfinished work of Christ as our Great High Priest in heaven). Then, when all was done, the leper was finally declared to be clean. Truly sin (of which leprosy is but a type) is a tenacious thing.

Devotion 13

Thou Shalt Remember

Deuteronomy 24:18–19

"Thou shalt remember that thou wast a bondman in Egypt, and the LORD thy God redeemed thee thence: therefore I command thee to do this thing. When thou cuttest down thine harvest in thy field, and hast forgot a sheaf in the field, thou shalt not go again to fetch it: it shall be for the stranger, for the fatherless, and for the widow."

The book of Deuteronomy should really be called *Down Memory Lane.* Two phrases run side by side through the book: "Thou shalt remember" and "Beware lest ye forget."

Here Moses calls upon God's people to remember three things.

They were to remember *their ruin*: "Thou shalt remember that thou wast a bondman in Egypt." This was John Newton's favorite text. He lived a wild and profligate life on the high seas as a slave trader. Eventually he sank so low as to actually become the slave of a slave, the slave of a woman who exulted in her power over him and made him even beg for his bread. He could never recall those days without a shudder. After his conversion he wrote out this text—"Thou shalt remember that thou wast a bondman (a slave) . . . and the LORD thy God redeemed thee." He put it on the mantelpiece of his study to remind him.

But, back to Israel's plight in Egypt. A slave! In Egypt! Indeed how the mighty had fallen! Proud Judah, crafty Levi, cruel Simeon, ambitious Ephraim—they were all slaves. They were all under the sentence of death, with no power to redeem themselves, still less to redeem their brothers. Such was the extent of their ruin.

Then, too, they were to remember *their redemption*: "The LORD thy God redeemed thee"— the Lord, Jehovah that is, the *God of Covenant,* the One who had entered into a contractual relationship with Abraham in what we now call the Abrahamic covenant. And what a covenant that is—an unconditional contract embracing the promulgation, protection, and promotion of Abraham's seed. "The Lord redeemed thee!"—He was faithful to His contract despite His people's unfaithfulness.

"The Lord thy *God* redeemed thee." God! Here the word is *Elohim*—God as the God of creation, the God who has power enough and to spare. What a God He is! He has power to endow an atom with energy enough to annihilate an island of the sea. The God who has power enough to fuel a hundred billion stars in a hundred billion galaxies and send them on prodigious journeys at unconceivable velocities across the vast reaches of space.

"The Lord thy *God* redeemed thee," Moses said. "Never forget it!" Rather, "Never forget *Him*."

Moreover, they were to remember *their responsibility*. They were to express their gratitude, not in sacrifices and offerings, not in rituals and religious observances, though, of course, such things had their place. They were to remember it by showing kindness to the poor, to the widow, to the stranger, and to the fatherless—especially at harvesttime.

God would have us to be ever mindful of the poor. He is mindful of them for when His own Son lived down here on earth, He was numbered among the poor. We should never forget it.

Devotion 14

Caleb

Joshua 14:6–15

The Jews divided old age into three stages. Age sixty to seventy was the "commencement" of old age. Age seventy to eighty was "hoary-headed" age. At eighty, one was said to be "well stricken in years." Caleb was eighty-five when he demanded his inheritance and asked to be given a haunted mountain where the sons of the Anakim ruled. It is never too late to dare something for God. Abraham was seventy-five when he left Ur. Moses was eighty when God met him at the burning bush. John was an old man when he wrote his books.

"I wholly followed the Lord," was Caleb's word to Joshua (Josh. 14:8). He had followed the Lord *fully*. He had been born in a ghetto in Goshen about the time Moses had fled from Egypt. Oh, how he longed for a Savior! When Moses came back as Israel's kinsman-redeemer, Caleb had become one of his devoted followers. He had been sheltered behind the blood of the Passover lamb. He had been baptized unto Moses in the cloud and in the sea. He had been gathered with God's people around the table in the wilderness. He had feasted on bread from heaven, drunk water from the riven rock, and smitten Amalek (a type of the flesh) with the edge of the sword. He had even been over Jordan. So, where others saw a diabolical foe, Caleb saw a defeated foe.

Caleb's name means "dog"; and like a faithful dog, he wholly followed the Master. He could say, "I have wholly followed the Lord."

Then, too, he followed the Lord *fearlessly*. Note *his calm assessment of the outlook*. The way ahead promised to be *arduous*. It was a mountain he claimed. Caleb knew it would be an uphill fight all the way. It promised to be *dangerous*, for the sons of the Anakim were there, a hybrid race of giants. It promised to be *tedious*, for the cities were great and fenced. They would have to be taken by long and stubborn siege. Such was his clear assessment of the outlook. But note, also, *his calm assurance of the outlook*: "If so be the Lord will be with me [He was counting on the Lord's *presence.*], then I shall be able to drive them out, as the Lord said [He was counting on the Lord's *promise.*]" (v. 12).

Finally, Caleb had followed the Lord *faithfully*. There were no stops and starts in his commitment, nothing but a steady walk with God.

Years ago, Alan Redpath, a well-known preacher and former pastor of Moody Church, was crossing the Atlantic on the *Queen Elizabeth*. He made friends with one of the ship's engineers. The man took him down to see the mighty engines roaring and pounding in the depths of the ship. Then he took him back to the stern of the boat, where the driveshafts throbbed and screamed as they turned the giant propellers that drove the mighty floating hotel through the water—all 83,000 tons of it.

Back in the chief engineer's cabin, Alan ventured a comment. "I suppose," he said, "those driveshafts and propellers must be going around at an enormous speed!"

"It's plain that you are no engineer!" replied the officer. "I could get those propellers going so fast, Alan, that they would just dig a big hole in the water, and the ship would come to a stop. I have forty-eight engineers under me on this ship," he added, "and they are constantly calculating the ratio between revolutions per minute in the engine room and *steadiness at the point of drive*."

Steadiness! That was the word! That is the word that sums up Caleb. He was steady. He wholly followed the Lord, come what may. May we do the same.

Devotion 15

Naomi Finds Grace

Ruth 1:6–17

The world, as represented by Moab, opened its arms to Elimelech the backslider. He settled down in that dark and dangerous place. He lost his sons to Moab. As Moab had once, years before, seduced the men of Israel with the women of Moab, so now Moab seduced the sons of Elimelech with the same bait. Elimelech's sons were quite content to live in Moab, to marry in Moab, and in the end to die in Moab and be buried in Moab. And so they did, far from God, their consciences silenced, their convictions, if they ever had any, seduced, and their days shortened.

Naomi lived through it all, growing more and more desolate, lonely, and embittered as time went on. Her only solace was that her two daughters-in-law respected her and treated her well. Ten years wore wearily away. Graves were dug. Husbands and sons were buried. And all about her the Moabites went about their business and carried on their dark religion as priests of Chemosh offered living children in the fires of their god. Ten weary years passed, and then a change came.

We think, first, of Naomi's *tidings*. She heard from home. The famine was over! The fields bore promise of a bumper harvest! God had been visiting His people! Revival had come! Naomi made up her mind. She would go home. Backsliding had beggared and embittered her, but her heart was still hungry for the place where God had put His name. She would go home and take her place once more with the people of God.

We think, also of Naomi's *testimony*. She told her two daughters-in-law of her decision. She was sick to death of Moab. She intended to get right with God, with the true and living God of her people. She would say "good-bye" to them. All backsliding had done for her was rob her and ruin her. *Mara* ("bitter") should be her true name, not *Naomi* ("pleasant"). Gone was the blessing associated with the name "Naomi" (Ruth

1:20). Instead had come the bitterness associated with the name "Mara." Such was her unpromising testimony.

Poor as that testimony was, however, it bore fruit. Both Ruth and Orpah were impressed by the sudden change in Naomi. They both declared that they would come as well. However, like the backslider she still was, Naomi tried to discourage them. "You would do better to stay in Moab," she said. "You'll never get remarried if you come with me. I can't think of a self-respecting Jew who would marry a Moabite." It was terrible advice. It should warn us never to take advice from a backslider. A backslider is a dangerous person no matter who or where that person is. Abraham's backsliding imperiled Sarah (Gen. 12:11–20). Lot's backsliding destroyed his family (Gen. 13:8–13; 19:1–38). Jonah's backsliding put others in peril (Jonah 1:4–16).

In Orpah's case, Naomi's words were all too successful. She took Naomi's advice and went back to the nightmare darkness of Moab, back to the demon gods of her people, and we read of her no more. Ever afterward, we can be sure, Naomi had Orpah's lost soul on her conscience. It would haunt her and grieve her beyond words.

But Ruth was made of sterner stuff. She had seen glimpses of God in Naomi. And she liked what she had seen. "I'm coming," she said. "I want to know more of your God and His people." And so she did. Thus God brought something good out of it after all—a precious soul, a woman who would find her place among God's redeemed people and help move forward the coming of the Christ of God.

Devotion 16

Ruth Finds Boaz

Ruth 2–4

When we first meet Ruth, she is in a far country, an alien from God and a stranger to grace. Unlike the Prodigal Son, she did not *burst* into the far country. He came there pursuing pleasure and wasting his substance with riotous living. Ruth was *born* in the far country, so she knew from her own experience what an empty place it was. To Ruth, the "far country" was Canaan, a longed-for land of life and rest where people worshiped the true and living God, not the fierce and filthy gods of Moab.

Perhaps she had dreamed of such a place in her younger days. If so, the place of her dreams was a faraway country, indeed, known to no one in Moab. If so, too, her meeting with one of Elimelech's sons must have given sudden form and substance to her dreams. For he had been born in that country. He and his parents could give it shape and form as well as a name—Canaan, the Promised Land.

So she married into this family and listened eagerly to the tales Naomi told and to the truths Elimelech taught, until the death of her husband faced her with the challenge of a change. When Naomi announced her decision to go back home to her people and her God, Ruth made up her mind. She would go with Naomi to the land of her dreams.

Then Boaz, the kinsman-redeemer, the mighty man of wealth, came into her life. Desperately poor, she took advantage of the land laws of Israel and went into the fields to glean. It so happened, we are told, that she chose a field that belonged to Boaz, a man she did not know but who was soon to fill her life.

We find her, then, in the *field of Boaz.* She had come a long way. Up to now she had never heard his name. She knew little of the Hebrew law of the kinsman-redeemer. Possibly Elimelech and Naomi had told her about Moses who had become a kinsman-redeemer to Israel. (Moses exemplifies redemption by *power*; Boaz depicts redemption by *purchase.*) Perhaps she had heard of these things from Naomi. Even so she would still not know how they could relate to her. But, at least, she was now in his field. And while Ruth knew little or nothing about these things, Boaz most certainly did.

Ruth must have been astonished to discover that Boaz knew all about her. More than that, he poured out his grace upon her, made provision for her, and sent her home laden down with good things.

Next, we find her at the *feet of Boaz.* "The man is near of kin unto us," Naomi said when Ruth arrived home bursting with news (Ruth 2:20). For she saw it at once! The law of the kinsman-redeemer opened every door. Naomi, back in fellowship with God's people, was now able to give good and godly advice to Ruth. "You must go to this man," she said, "you must put yourself at his feet and ask to be redeemed. You must invoke the Law and ask Boaz to marry you." Boaz did not need to be reminded of the Law! He was already in love with Ruth. Love, not law, would guide his steps now. So Ruth came to Boaz, just as she was, in all her need and put herself at his feet.

Finally, we see her in the *family of Boaz.* The claims of the Law had to be met, especially the rules and regulations connected with the role and responsibilities of a kinsman-redeemer. There was no way Ruth could fulfill the Law's demands. The Law legislated against her in a most forceful way since she was a Moabite. But Boaz could meet the Law's demands, and he did. Then he paid the price of Ruth's redemption and purchased both her person and her late husband's property. Then Boaz married her and put her in his family and gave her a living link to Christ. All of this, of course, and much more beside, Jesus does for us.

Devotion 17

Ruth Finds Rest

Ruth 3:3

Orpah sought rest in Moab, but she sought it there in vain. Rest is centered in a person not a place, and Orpah never found that person. Ruth did. She met Boaz, and her life was never the same again. It was Naomi, the restored backslider, who taught Ruth how to find her rest in Boaz.

First, there had to be *cleansing.* "Wash thyself," she said. Obviously Ruth could not go to Boaz bathed in perspiration from a hard day's gleaning in the field. Gleaning was hot, hard work. It involved a great deal of physical activity—bending and stretching, cutting and gathering—all through the burden and heat of the day. She needed to be cleansed from all that.

"Wash thyself." When God sought to convey to the Hebrew people the fact of sin's defilement, He did so by means of the tabernacle. At one end He sat in the Holy of Holies, enthroned in unimpeachable righteousness and holiness. At the other end stood the guilty sinner. Between them stood the brazen altar and the brazen laver, *blood* and *water.*

A sinner could approach God only by way of the altar and the laver. He would arrive first at the brazen altar to present his sin offering or his trespass offering. Blood was shed. This recognized the fact that there had to be a *radical* cleansing from sin. Next (if he was a priest), he came to the brazen laver, which was made from the mirrors of the women. He saw at once that he had been defiled in his walk, even going that short way. He needed a *renewed* cleansing from sin. He needed what Paul would later call, "the washing of water by the word" (Eph. 5:26). "Wash yourself," said Naomi to Ruth. And so she did.

Next, came *consecration.* "Anoint thee," Naomi said. Anointing, in both the Old and New Testaments, points us to the person and work of the Holy Spirit. There must be no odor of the flesh about us when we come to our heavenly Boaz seeking rest. There must be a fragrance of

God about us. Mary of Bethany could tell us about that. She brought her costly perfume and used that precious ointment to anoint the Lord Jesus. Instantly the whole house was filled with fragrance (John 12:1–3). Likewise, Ruth was taught to come to Boaz bearing the fragrance of one anointed. It advertised her presence in a bold but silent, unmistakable, and pleasing way.

Finally, there was *character*: "Put thy raiment upon thee," said Naomi. This raiment evidently was not what she wore to work, stained with sweat, drenched with perspiration. No, indeed! This raiment was fresh and fit for the master's house. In the symbolism of the Bible, raiment speaks of character. We are to "put off" the old man and his deeds and "put on" the new man. Ruth's true character was already known to Boaz. He had already acknowledged her to be a virtuous woman.

Thus prepared, Ruth came to Boaz, and he responded at once. Before long, he took her to himself and made her his very own. All of this points us to Christ. When we are united to Him, we can sing in the words of the gospel hymn:

> I came to Jesus as I was,
> Weary and worn and sad;
> I found in Him a resting place,
> And He has made me glad.[1]

---

1. Horatius Bonar, "I Heard the Voice of Jesus Say," 1846.

Devotion 18

Boaz Finds a Way

Ruth 3:11–4:13

Love always finds a way. As the hymn writer puts it:

> Love found a way to redeem my soul.
> Love found a way that could make me whole.
> Love took my Lord to the cross of shame.
> Love found a way—oh bless His holy name.[1]

"Love never faileth." *That,* says the Holy Spirit, is the nature of love.

There can be no doubt that Boaz loved Ruth, right from the start, even before he actually met her there in the harvest field. "All the city of my people doth know that thou art a virtuous woman," he said (Ruth 3:11). He knew all about her. His heart was already stirred.

And then he met her. The "servant that was set over the reapers" told Boaz who she was (2:6). In the Old Testament an unnamed servant is often a type of the Holy Spirit. It was this unnamed servant who made the introduction, that momentous face-to-face meeting at which Boaz's heart went out to Ruth. He gave her ample evidence of the state of his heart. He gave her an ephah of grain, ten times what she needed. He would marry her—in spite of the obstacles! And there were four of them, and formidable obstacles they were. But love found a way.

The first obstacle was the fact of a *cursed race.* Ruth was a Moabite, and the Moabites were a people under the curse of God. The reason was historical (Num. 22–25; Deut. 23:3–6). When the Hebrews reached the Moabite frontier, on their way from Egypt to Canaan, the Moabites opposed them. In fact, they hired a Mesopotamian psychic to come and curse them. When that failed, they corrupted them and then looked for God to curse them for their sin. God punished the fallen Israelites, indeed; but He also brought a curse down upon the Moabite race. But

1. Ava B. Christiansen, "Wonderful Love That Rescued Me," 1915.

that was only part of it. The curse of the Law upon the Moabite people was but the *fruit.* The *root* of the curse went much deeper and ran back some 550 years or so. The father of Moab was Lot. Moab was the son incestuously conceived by Lot's oldest daughter on the hills overlooking the smoldering ruins of Sodom, and his godless descendants (the Moabites) became Israel's determined foes.

But there was another obstacle for Boaz. It was the obstacle of a *condemning rule,* for the Law legislated against the Moabite: "An Ammonite or Moabite shall not enter into the congregation of the LORD; even to their tenth generation shall they not enter . . . for ever. . . . Thou shalt not seek their peace nor their prosperity all thy days for ever" (Deut. 23:3, 6). That was indeed a formidable obstacle. Only the bringing into operation of a higher law (the law of the kinsman-redeemer) could find a way around it.

Then, too, there was the obstacle of a *closer relative.* Boaz had to be very careful in working his way around this obstacle. Two issues were involved. First, there was the matter of the *property* (the property of Elimelech, which was in limbo now that his sons, Mahlon and Chilion, were also dead). The nearer kinsman was eager to gain possession of that property.

Then, suddenly, Boaz raised the other issue, the matter of the *person.* The nearer kinsman could not have the property without the person. If he wanted to acquire the property, he also would have to wed the widow Ruth. He backed off in a hurry. He certainly did not want to wed a cursed Moabite. The last thing he wanted was to mar his family tree and spoil his hope of becoming an ancestor of Christ by introducing Moabite blood into his ancestral line. Boaz had no such scruples. His family tree was already "marred." His mother was the Canaanite harlot, Rahab.

Finally, there was the obstacle of a *costly requirement.* As kinsman-redeemer he would be obliged to buy both the person and the property of Ruth. Redemption was a costly business. Boaz, however, was both able and willing to pay the price for he was a "mighty man of wealth" (Ruth 2:1), and he loved the Moabite widow with all his heart. So love found a way. The obstacles were swept aside, Boaz married the Moabite, and the stage was set for the coming of Christ.

Devotion 19

Samuel the Prophet

1 Samuel 1:25; 3:20; 7:15–17

Samuel's name is listed among the giants of the faith in Hebrews 11. He was the last of the judges and the first of the prophets. Compared with others of his day, he was a veritable spiritual giant. He was a far greater threat to the Philistines, the hereditary foes of Israel, than Samson ever was, for all of Samson's exploits and practical jokes. Samuel towered head and shoulders above King Saul and helped launch the illustrious David on his triumphant way.

We begin with Samuel's *mother.* Hannah was a remarkable woman, a woman full of faith, able to lay hold of God until assured her barrenness would be turned into blessedness. Included in her pleas for a son was a promise to God to give that son back to God. When the little boy was born, she called him Samuel, which means "asked of God." The name was to remind her, when the temptation came to keep him, that he was not *hers* but was His. He was God's.

Then there was his *mentor,* the old priest, Eli, a man who became a second father to Samuel. Eli had done very badly in raising his own sons, but he did exceedingly well in raising Samuel. Soon all Israel knew that a new prophet had arisen, one who knew God and who, young as he was, could speak for God. It was Eli who taught and trained the boy, but it was his mother who prayed for him, for her growing "Asked of God," now wholly given to God.

We think, too, of Samuel's *ministry*. He lived in a very dark day. There was no king in Israel; and there was no prophet, except himself, to speak for God. The priesthood was in a shambles, and the period of the judges was coming to its inglorious end. The people had been on a seesaw for centuries, up and down, up and down, getting nowhere and ringed in by fierce and implacable foes. The knowledge of the true and living God lingered in the land, but a revival was needed. And Samuel was the man to bring it.

We find that when *the will of God was to be sought,* it was Samuel who travailed in prayer to ascertain when and where and how this or that or the other thing should be done. It was Samuel who wrestled with God over the matter of the constitutional change of Israel from a theocracy into a monarchy. It was Samuel who wrestled with God over the matter of terminating Saul's infant dynasty and transferring the kingdom to David.

Moreover, when *the wars of God were to be fought,* it was Samuel who stood in the gap. It was Samuel who fought the Philistines and proclaimed his "Ebenezer" saying, "Hitherto hath the Lord helped us" (I Sam. 7:12). Never again, after his last, spectacular victory, did the Philistines dare invade Israel in the days of Samuel. He was a greater man than Samson after all.

Then, too, when *the Word of God was to be taught,* it was Samuel who taught it. He became Israel's first prophet. Soon all Israel, from Dan to Beersheba, knew that Samuel was established to be a prophet of the Lord. He established a teaching itinerary. He traveled to Bethel, to Gilgal, to Mizpeh, and back to Ramah in circuit, judging Israel and trying to bring Israel back to the book.

Finally, full of years, the aged prophet died; and all Israel wept. And well they might, for such men are rare. They occur in every generation, but generally they stand alone, giants in the earth. "Time would fail me to tell of . . . Samuel," is the Holy Spirit's last word about Samuel (Heb. 11:32). And so it would. We shall have to wait, therefore, till time shall be no more to hear the rest of this story.

Devotion 20

The Road to Endor

1 Samuel 28:1–25

It was a long, perilous, evil road from Ramah, where the prophet Samuel lived, to the place where the witch of Endor lived. Of course, she had no business living there, or anywhere else, for the Mosaic Law decreed that witches be put to death. But live she did, and the path to her door was the path King Saul trod. It took him forty years to get there, and it cost him dearly when he did. The milestones he passed on that long, winding, downward road still mark out the way. There are a half dozen of them all told.

The first milestone marked Saul's *undeveloped potential* (I Sam. 11–12). He seems to have cut an impressive figure in his younger days and was chosen by the people to be king because he looked so very much a man. And he started well enough, rescuing the city of Jabesh-gilead from the power of the Ammonite king. The victory encouraged the aging Samuel to retire, for Saul, it seemed, had the potential to be a good king. Sadly, Saul allowed it to all go to waste.

The second milestone marked Saul's *unpardonable presumption* (I Sam. 13). War broke out with the Philistines. The aged Samuel promised to come and bless Saul's men and he set a time for doing so. The appointed week wore on. Men began to desert, and still Samuel tarried. Saul felt he was losing his army and became impatient, so he took it on himself to act as priest. If Samuel wanted to dillydally, then that was too bad for Samuel. Saul intruded into the priests' exclusive domain and sacrificed his offering himself. It never seemed to occur to him that God was testing him by Samuel's divinely appointed delay. The smoke was still ascending from his altar when Samuel appeared. He denounced Saul and told him he had forfeited the kingdom. Moreover, God had Saul's successor in mind, "a man after God's own heart."

The third milestone marked Saul's *untimely procrastination* (I Sam. 14). The desultory war with the Philistines needed to be brought to a head, but Saul had no stomach for fighting Philistines. So Jonathan, Saul's son, took the lead. What was King Saul doing? He was tarrying, we are told, in the uttermost part of Gibeah, under a pomegranate tree. He was wasting his time. He had failed once by presumption. He failed now by procrastination.

The fourth milestone marked his *unsatisfactory performance* (I Sam. 15). The time had come to visit God's judgment on the Amalekites for their bitter hostility to the people of God. "Slay utterly," was God's command. They must deal with this relentless foe once and for all. (In Bible typology Amalek represents the flesh. God tells us to deal with it as drastically as Saul was to deal with Amalek.)

Saul triumphed, indeed, but he spared Agag the Amalekite king and the best of the flocks and herds. Saul had failed another test. Samuel angrily brushed off Saul's excuses. He called him a rebel. "*Rebellion is as the sin of witchcraft,*" said Samuel, with a prophetic eye on the future and final fate of King Saul. Truly this was a notable milestone. The incident marked the end of any further divine validity to Saul's reign and the beginning of a life of crime.

The fifth milestone marked his *undisguised paralysis* (I Sam. 17). The Philistines declared war and put forth their giant, Goliath. He challenged Saul (a giant himself) to come and fight him man to man. Saul shook in his shoes. He was so petrified with terror that he let a young lad, David by name, go and fight the giant for him. The people soon sized up that act of cowardice.

The sixth milestone marked his *unremitting persecution* of the one who had taken his place in the valley of death. No less than twenty-four times King Saul tried to kill David. One black day, he massacred a whole company of priests, accusing them of high treason because their leader had given David some small loaves of bread and Goliath's sword, to help him out of the country.

And so, at last, King Saul came to Endor, where lived a witch. Samuel was dead. Heaven was silent when Saul prayed. And once again the Philistines were preparing to invade. The new, puppet high priest Saul had installed could get no answer from God, either, when he tried to intercede. So Saul turned to the witch. He had knocked on heaven's door in vain. He decided to knock instead on the door of hell. God opened that door suddenly and startlingly. Instead of the witch's familiar spirit showing up, the dead Samuel did—to sentence Saul to death. So, having opened a normally barred and bolted door, God pushed Saul through it to a lost eternity.

Centuries earlier the hireling prophet, Balaam, said: "Let me die the death of the righteous, and let my last end be like his!" (Num. 23:10). He, too, died under the judgment of God. We cannot die the death of the righteous if we do not live the life of the righteous. And *that* King Saul never did.

Devotion 21

As an Angel of God

2 Samuel 19:27–30

"My lord the king is as an angel of God." The words were spoken by poor, broken Mephibosheth, who had been maliciously slandered by Ziba, his self-seeking scoundrel of a servant. David, sad to say, more than half believed the tale that Ziba had told him, that Mephibosheth, grandson of King Saul, was planning to turn the Absalom rebellion to his own gain. But now the time had come for Mephibosheth to speak.

"You sought me," he said. "You sought me!" And that was so. "Is there yet any that is left of the house of Saul, that I may show him kindness for Jonathan's sake?" David had inquired (2 Sam. 9:1).

Ziba had told him about Jonathan's son Mephibosheth, lame in both his feet, dwelling afar off, in virtual hiding, in hourly fear for his life. Mephibosheth had been the victim of a fall. His estates were all gone. He was living at Lo-Debar, "the place of no pasture," a dry and barren place indeed. And he had no claim on the king. His grandfather had been King Saul, a man who feared and hated David and had tried on some two dozen occasions to murder him. So Mephibosheth was in a sorry plight. He is a prime Old Testament type of the sinner, one who has no standing before God and no claim upon Him at all.

David sought him out, however, determined to bring him back to himself. Mephibosheth remembered that.

"You saved me," he said. "You saved me!" And so he had. It was David's idea, just as the salvation of a sinner is all God's idea, not ours. All the initiative is His.

> He saw me ruined by the fall,
> Yet loved me notwithstanding all;
> He saved me from my lost estate,
> His lovingkindness, O how great.[1]

---

1. Samuel Medley, "Awake, My Soul, to Joyful Lays," 1782.

What must have been the feelings of Mephibosheth that day when, hobbling around the barren barnyard there in Lo-Debar, he looked up and saw horsemen on the horizon arrayed in the uniform of the palace guard.

"They've found me!" he said to himself. "They'll kill me. David has every cause to put me to death." And he plied his wretched crutches in a hopeless attempt to escape. The soldiers caught him soon enough and confronted him.

"Our lord the king," said the captain of the guard, "summons you to his presence. He wants to show you the kindness of God." Good news indeed! Grace, not wrath! How like David! And how like our Lord Jesus Christ! We can be sure that Mephibosheth wasted no time in responding to the royal call.

"You seated me," he said. "You seated me!" And so he had. For David restored all Mephibosheth's lost estates and treated him as one of the king's sons, giving him a place at his own table in Jerusalem. All this Mephibosheth remembered. He had come! He had hidden his poor, lame feet under the table of the king. Every day with David was sweeter than the day before.

And now it was his turn to speak. "My lord the king," he said, "is as an angel of God." As for Ziba and the property, let him have it all. What need did Mephibosheth have for *land*? He had his *Lord*. That was enough for him.

Devotion 22

An Almost Empty Barrel

1 Kings 17:8–16

The barrel belonged to a widow. She was not even a Hebrew widow. The Law of Moses made provision for Hebrew widows and orphans, but this woman had no such resource. Her case was desperate. All that remained to her, all that stood between her and starvation in a cold, pitiless world, was an almost empty barrel—almost empty but not quite.

The prophet Elijah had been sent to meet this widow. He had been staying by a brook, but it had run dry and God had directed him to go to Zarephath, an outpost of Zidon, where he would be cared for by a widow. Elijah's reactions were probably mixed. "A widow?" he might have exclaimed. "I wonder if she is young or old, good-looking or plain, rich or poor? But Zidon! Why *that* is where Jezebel comes from. Her father, Ethbaal, is king of the Zidonians; and that could be dangerous for me. Jezebel is scouring the land to lay her hands on me." But Elijah had not become a prince of prophets by running away from danger. So off he went to find this widow. Centuries later Jesus reminded His neighbors at Nazareth that there were many widows in Israel in the days of Elijah, but God did not send Elijah to any of them. He sent him to a Gentile widow. Thus Elijah became the first prophet to the Gentiles.

We can picture their first encounter. The widow he met, at last, was evidently poor, and she had a child tied to her apron strings. Probably the prophet was far from impressed. "Excuse me, ma'am," he might have said, "do you know of any rich widows around here? I am a prophet. God has told me I will find a widow from these parts who will give me room and board."

"I'm that widow."

"Is that so? Well, please bring me some water; and I am hungry, so please bring me something to eat."

"All I have is a handful of meal in a barrel, just enough for me and my son. I am going home to make a small biscuit. I shall share it with my son, and then we shall starve to death."

A handful of meal! That was all. Of course, it all depends on whose hand is full. It so happened, in this case, that the hand that was full was the hand of God, the hand that holds the prairies. That hand could never fail.

There are three factors in the equation of this interlude in Elijah's ministry. First, there was handful of *meal* in her near-empty barrel. That meal spoke of the Christ. The second great offering of the Mosaic Law was the *meal* offering. It pictured the sinless humanity of the Lord Jesus, pure, even, crushed beneath the millstones and fit to be offered to God.

But this widow had something else, something that almost gets overlooked. She had a little oil in her flask. That oil would blend with the meal and make the dough for a small cake. The oil speaks of the Holy Spirit. The Holy Spirit is part of everything Jesus said, and did, and was. He was conceived of the Holy Spirit, filled with the Holy Spirit, anointed by the Holy Spirit, and offered in sacrifice to God through the Holy Spirit. As the flour and the oil were blended together, so the Son and the Spirit were blended together.

There was one other factor in this Old Testament equation of Christ. The woman was holding *two sticks.* The two sticks, surely, represent the cross. It takes two sticks to make a *cross,* no more, no less. The woman had a firm grip on what she needed—*Christ,* the Christ of the meal offering; the *Comforter,* the oil in a vessel; and the *cross.* They saw her through to the end.

That nearly empty barrel was never quite empty. That oil was just enough for each and every day, and Calvary took care of it all. God does not ask much of us when we first come into contact with Him in our deep need. But He does insist that we have some grasp on the Christ, the Comforter, and the cross. That will see us through.

Devotion 23

OBADIAH OF SAMARIA

1 KINGS 18:1–16

It is Obadiah's lasting misfortune that when we take his measure, he is not standing alone, by himself. Otherwise we might have thought him a giant. But unfortunately for Obadiah, he is always standing alongside Elijah, a giant indeed. Elijah not only made poor Obadiah look like a pygmy, but he also treated him with scant respect. But we are letting our story run away with us.

Let us begin with Obadiah's *testimony*. The Holy Spirit says that "Obadiah feared the LORD greatly." Just the same, Obadiah was afraid of King Ahab and even more afraid of Jezebel. The two of them were a formidable pair. Jezebel was determined to stamp out the worship of Jehovah in Israel and had imported more than eight hundred pagan priests and prophets to accomplish her end. Obadiah was more afraid of her then he was of God. Small wonder. Even Elijah ran away from her.

Obadiah was an official at Ahab's court. He ran the royal household. He knew how matters stood. He was afraid of Ahab. Ahab was afraid of Jezebel. Jezebel was afraid of nobody.

Though Obadiah's fear of God was flawed, the Holy Spirit nevertheless bears witness to the fact that "Obadiah feared the LORD greatly."

There were one hundred Hebrew prophets in Israel whom Jezebel wanted put to death, and it was a criminal offense to help them. They had gone into hiding, and Jezebel's secret police scoured the country looking for them. There was one man who knew where they were—Obadiah. He had hidden them. Moreover he took advantage of his position as Ahab's steward to smuggle food and drink to them. God honored him for that. Such was his testimony. He had faith. But he lived with fear as well.

Next, we see Obadiah's *task*. He was ordered by Ahab to search the whole country in the hope of finding enough grass to feed the royal horses and mules—a well-nigh hopeless task. The drought Elijah had imposed on Israel had lasted now for three and a half years, and the land was bare. Obadiah did not have the courage to point out to Ahab that it was *his* apostasy that was responsible for the state of affairs in Israel. He went off on his hopeless errand.

And then he met Elijah. He could hardly believe his eyes. There was an enormous price on Elijah's head. He was the object of a massive nationwide manhunt. "Go and tell Ahab I'm here," he said. This brings us to Obadiah's *terror.* "Why," he said, "Ahab's police are looking for you everywhere! Ahab's ambassadors have agreements with all the surrounding countries to extradite you should you surface in one of them. This is a trick. I'll go and get the king, and the moment my back is turned the Spirit of God will whisk you away, and I'll be left to face the fury of Ahab and Jezebel. What have I sinned that you want to betray me like that? Is this my reward for hiding those prophets?"

Well, Obadiah had his day in the spotlight. Elijah lived in it. "Obadiah," we read, "went to meet Ahab." And that is the last we hear of him. "Obadiah went to meet Ahab." Then we read: "And Ahab went to meet Elijah." There lies the difference. Obadiah was ruled by caution; Elijah was ruled by conviction. Obadiah was one of those seven thousand the Lord talked about, men who had not bowed the knee to Baal. That's the best we can say about him. Elijah took heaven by storm. Obadiah limped along the highway home. Still, God gives him credit where credit is due. He "feared the Lord greatly"—far more than most of his countrymen did. God writes it into His Book. What does He write into His Book about us?

Devotion 24

"What Doest Thou Here, Elijah?"

1 Kings 19:1–16

"What doest thou here, Elijah?" The question is asked twice in less than half a dozen verses. And the prophet gives the same sad reply both times.

It is often helpful, in opening up a verse or so of Scripture, to go through the passage, putting the emphasis on a different word each time—"What *doest* thou here Elijah?" Well, of course, he was doing nothing, just sitting at Sinai feeling sorry for himself. "What doest *thou* here, Elijah?" He, of all people! The man who had just come from Carmel and a glorious, miraculous victory! "What doest thou *here,* Elijah?" Why was he sitting in the shadow of Sinai, forty days' journey from the sphere of duty, as though more edicts from the holy mount could help either him or his people? "What doest thou here, *Elijah*?" His name is a combination of the two primary names for God—Elohim and Jehovah—the God of creation, omnipotent in power; the God of covenant, matchless in grace. What was a man with a name like that doing at Sinai when he should have been in Samaria?

Elijah, fearless before Ahab, had fled from Jezebel. Now the reaction had set in. The day after a great victory is always a time of danger for the child of God because Satan always counterattacks. Elijah, with Jezebel's threats curdling his blood, had fled a day's journey into the wilderness. He felt himself friendless and alone. Already the baying of the bloodhounds could be heard, sounding across the desert.

His flight appalled him. "I am not better than my fathers," he moaned. "Let me die!" he said. "Come and dine," God replied. God knew His man was exhausted physically and spiritually. "Let me die!" That was self-pity speaking. After all, if Elijah had *really* wanted to die, all he needed to do was let Jezebel know where he was! In any case, God had something far better than martyrdom in store for Elijah.

So an angel came, cooked the prophet's supper for him, and then his breakfast. Restored physically, the prophet went in the strength of those two meals for forty days, all the way to Sinai. Now, far from where he should have been, Elijah had a fresh fit of the sulks. God challenged him: "What doest thou here, Elijah?" "I, even I, am the only one left," he moaned—something that was obviously not true. There was Obadiah and his hidden prophets to start with. They may not have been calling down fire, but they had certainly not bowed the knee to Baal either.

God had revealed Himself as a *sympathizing* God. Now He reveals Himself as a *sufficient* God.

First, we see the mount of God: "Go forth, and stand upon the mount before the LORD," God said. Elijah's hero Moses had climbed that awesome peak of Sinai no less than seven times in receiving the Law. Now it was Elijah's turn. Up he went. And there he stood, hiding from a hurricane, from a terrifying earthquake, and from a flaming fire. Each of these awesome exhibits of God's power passed before the shaken prophet, but God was not in any of them. They were tools God had at His disposal. He was just reminding His runaway prophet that He had all kinds of instruments with which to fight Jezebel, if He wanted to use them. So, why be afraid of Jezebel?

"Yes, Elijah," God said, "I can tear, but I much prefer to teach." So the forces of nature were all replaced by a still small voice. "Yes, my child, I can perform miracles. You ought to know that. I loaned you My weapon of fire on Carmel. But miracles are not all that effective. It is My Word that produces the best results. The wind can blow, the fire can burn, and the earthquake can break; but My Word, still and small to your mortal ears, is 'quick, and powerful, and sharper than any twoedged sword'" (Heb 4:12).

After all this, God asked the prophet again: "What doest thou here, Elijah?" "I'm the only one left. They want to kill me," said Elijah. Still full of self-pity the prophet repeated word-for-word what he had said before.

"That's enough!" God said. "Go and anoint Elisha to replace you. That's *one* you didn't know about, whose knees have never bowed to Baal. And, by the way, I have seven thousand faithful saints who have not bowed to Baal. You don't know any of them. I know all of them."

But God is very kind. He did not answer Elijah's plea to die. Not a bit of it! He allowed him to train his successor. Then, blessed be God, He sent a chariot of fire and an angel escort to carry Elijah straight into the glory! How good and gracious a God He is.

Devotion 25

THE MANTLE OF ELIJAH

2 KINGS 2:13–14

Down it came, down from on high, down to the ground to lie in a heap at the feet of Elisha, Elijah's colleague, servant, and friend. Elisha picked it up. It was the seal of a new covenant between him and the ascended master in heaven. He had prayed for a double portion of the master's spirit. "Keep your eye on me, then," said Elijah. That was what Elisha had done. Now he had the mantle of the man in the glory.

Elisha saw something few have ever seen. He saw a living man caught up through the clouds. There had come a mighty rushing wind such as later came at Pentecost. There had come a chariot and horses of fire. Heaven had touched earth for an instant, there at Jordan, the river of death; and the master was gone. All that remained was a mantle, still warm from the touch of a living man, now caught up into heaven. The crack in the space-time dimension closed, and Elisha stood there alone.

How long Elisha stood there gazing up into heaven we do not know. But presently he brought his gaze back down to earth; and there it was—a mantle, the seal of the new covenant, the earnest of his inheritance. It was now his. And with it came the double portion he had desired. That mantle marked him out as a firstborn son. He picked it up, and the spirit of the master in heaven clothed the body of the disciple on earth. He would walk worthy of his lord. He would be fruitful in every good work. He would increase in the knowledge of God. But let us come back to that mantle.

The mantle of Elijah is mentioned four times. The first time it is associated with the *paradox* of the man of God (1 Kings 19:13). For Elijah, mighty man of God that he was, had feet of clay. He was a man subject to like passions as we are. We find him on Horeb, the Mount of God, far from where he belonged. God ministered gently to him. He revealed Himself in the fury of the wind and in the forces of the earthquake and in the fierceness of the fire. Elijah hid in the cave as all nature rumbled, roared, and rolled about him. Then came the still small voice. Elijah ventured out, his face wrapped in his mantle, and self-pitying still. We see the man who could call down fire sulking like a schoolboy. Alas, there would be no more Carmels after this. The paradox remains. The greatest man on earth was overcome by passions such as overthrow the weakest of people. God, most assuredly, does not whitewash the heroes of the faith.

The second time the mantle is mentioned it shows us the *personality* of the man of God (I Kings 19:19). There goes Elisha following his plow. Here comes Elijah, mantle in hand. The prophet throws the mantle over the plowman and so great is the power and charisma of Elijah that the successful businessman gives up all to follow him. Of course there wasn't a man, woman, boy, or girl from the king on his throne to the mendicant on the city streets, who had not heard of Elijah or been touched by the force of his personality.

The next time we see that mantle it reminds us of the *power* of a man of God (2 Kings 2:8). One flick of that mantle over Jordan's wave, and the waters fled. There was more power in the hem of that garment than in all the robes in King Ahab's house.

We see that mantle one more time, and it reminds us of the *pilgrimage* of a man of God. For when his earthly pathway was ended, Elijah stepped into a whirlwind and was gone. He would need the mantle no more. He passed it on to his heir. The new young prophet wore that mantle with all the authority of the one to whom it had formerly belonged.

The Lord expects the same of us. We are Christ's heirs to the Holy Spirit. We wear the Lord's mantle of power. The pilgrim church moves on through time, the mantle of the Spirit of God being the guarantee that God's will will be done on earth, even as it is in heaven.

Devotion 26

Why? But!

Psalm 22:1–6

Psalm 22 was written by David a thousand years before the birth of Christ. It contains no less than thirty-three distinct prophecies that were all literally fulfilled at Calvary. Who, but God, could so foretell the future? This psalm, for instance, records Emmanuel's orphan cry, that great cry of desolation that rang during the midday-midnight darkness that wrapped around Him in His agony on the cross.

We know that David was the human author of this psalm; but that only deepens the mystery because, though David knew what it was to suffer, his suffering never approximated the sufferings described here. The Holy Spirit simply took what could only have been hyperbole in David's case and transformed it into prophecy when David wrote it down.

The suffering Savior felt Himself abandoned by both God and man. We note the great gulf that separated Him from an *all-holy God* (vv. 1–3). "My God, my God, why hast thou forsaken me?" He asked. "Why art thou so far from helping me, and from the words of my roaring?" The Hebrew word for "roaring" is used for the roar of a lion and also for the cry of an animal in pain.

"Why? Why?" He cried, but there was no answer. Then the suffering Savior changed the word "why" to the word "but." He said, "But thou art holy!" That was it! The amazing and awesome mystery is that He was made sin for us. He did not become sinful, perish the thought! He became *sin* and "tasted death." A whole eternity was sandwiched into that dreadful period of time on the cross that began with the sixth hour and ended with the ninth hour. During that period total darkness held the whole land in its grip and Jesus experienced the ultimate terror of the lost, the horror of being left, in the dark, abandoned by God.

There was also the great gulf that separated Him from *all holy people* (vv. 4–6). Others cried and were heard. Abraham cried! Moses cried! David cried! God heard them. Jesus cried, and there was no reply.

Again the suffering Savior found a use for that little word *but.* "But," He said, "I am a worm, and no man." Who can plumb the depths of *that*? We could have understood it had He said He was a lion or a lamb. But a *worm*? We count a worm as being very low indeed in our scale of things. We forget that in God's sovereign dealings with Jonah, the worm was as necessary as the wind and the great fish. Just the same, we don't think much of worms! That is why we are so startled to hear the Savior say, "I am a worm."

The Lord, however, did not use the word for an ordinary worm. On the contrary, He made reference to the crimson crocus, which, when crushed, yielded the scarlet dye. It was a fitting type of the stricken Christ we see on Calvary, "dying, crushed beneath the lead of the wrath and curse of God." Well might the hymn writer say:

O make me understand it
Help me to take it in;
What it meant for Thee, the Holy One
To take away my sin.[1]

---

1. Katharine A. M. Kelly, "O Make Me Understand It."

Devotion 27

The Lord Is My Shepherd

Psalm 23

This is everybody's psalm. First, we are in the glen, then in the gorge, and finally, we are in the glory. The psalm tells us about the fold, about the foe, and about the future. It gives us the threefold secret of happiness. It begins with *the secret of a happy life.* Our Shepherd takes care of all of our needs. He takes care of all our *secular* needs. He leads us beside the still waters and into the green pastures. And He takes care of all our *spiritual* needs. He "restores our soul" and gives us needed righteousness. "He brings back my soul" is the way one translation renders it. And, at what cost! As the old hymn puts it,

> But none of the ransomed ever knew
> How deep were the waters crossed;
> Nor how dark was the night that
>   the Lord passed thro'
> Ere He found His sheep that was lost.[1]

The psalm continues with *the secret of a happy death.* We come now in the psalm to the valley of the shadow of death. We notice at once that there is a dramatic change in the pronouns. Up to now the psalmist has been saying: "He! He! He!" He has been talking *about* the Shepherd. Now He says, "Thou! Thou! Thou!" As the dark valley looms, the Shepherd comes closer. Now the psalmist is no longer talking about Him but is talking to Him.

And, behold, the threatening valley turns out to be no more than the valley of the *shadow* of death. The shadow of a dog cannot bite. The shadow of a sword cannot kill. The shadow of death cannot harm the child of God.

---

1. Elizabeth C. Clephane, "The Ninety and Nine," 1868.

Where there is a shadow, however, there has to be a substance. We discover that the substance of death is very close by, right there in the previous psalm—"My God, My God, why hast thou forsaken me?" That, indeed, is the substance of death: to be forsaken by God forever.

But there is something else, too. Where there is a shadow, there also has to be a light. It is the light shining on the substance that casts the shadow.

Some years ago I heard a letter read in church. It had just been received from a beloved medical missionary, who was dying of leukemia. He wrote: "David, in Psalm 23, talks about the valley of the shadow of death. Fellow saints of God, I have come into the valley. *But there is no shadow.* On the contrary, I have found that 'the path of the just is as the shining light, that shineth more and more unto the perfect day' (Prov. 4:18)." That is the secret of a happy death.

Finally, we have here *the secret of a happy eternity.* "I will dwell in the house of the Lord for ever." That is David's final offering.

Harriet Beecher Stowe, who wrote *Uncle Tom's Cabin,* perhaps did more to strike the shackles off America's slaves than any other person. In one of many dramatic scenes, she shows us poor Uncle Tom in the merciless hands of the cruel Simon Legree. The malicious slave owner was determined to break the will of the kindly Uncle Tom. When he refused to be cruel to the other slaves, even when commanded to thrash them by Legree's direct command, Legree threatened him with torture. "How would you like to have a slow fire built around you, Tom?" he said. "I know you can do many cruel things, Master," said Uncle Tom. "You can even kill me. But there's *all eternity to come after that.*" That was the heavenly vision that filled the soul of Uncle Tom with bliss and the soul of Simon Legree with terror.

F. W. Boreham reminds us of what old Rabbi Duncan used to say to his students at the turn of the year: "Gentlemen," he would say, "your friends will be wishing you a happy New Year. Your old Rabbi wishes you *a happy eternity.*" Jesus does better than that. He *assures* us a happy eternity.

Devotion 28

Angels' Food

Psalm 78:24–25

It never occurs to us that angels eat, still less that God would take royal dainties from their bountiful board on high and pour them out to mortal beings in hunger in a howling wilderness on a remote island planet in space called Earth. Yet this is what happened. God gave them "the corn of heaven." He gave them "angels' food." And that wondrous "bread from heaven" not only satisfied their hunger but was also a type of Jesus Himself, the Bread of God upon whom we feed as we wend our way through the wilderness of this world to the Promised Land above.

The story of the manna, as it was called, begins with *the discontent of the people.* They were a people recently redeemed from the house of bondage and from the sentence of death. They had been redeemed by power, put under the blood, baptized unto Moses in the sea, gathered to the living God, and were moving homewards. But they were hungry, and the wilderness had nothing to offer; just as the world has nothing to offer our hungry souls. So the people murmured and complained. They thought nostalgically of how well they were fed on onions, leeks, and garlic in Egypt. They conveniently forgot the toil, the sweat, the tears, the lash, the scourge, and the genocidal law that destined their young to sure and certain death. And they murmured against Moses and against God.

Then came *the discovery of the people.* They awoke one morning to a world turned white as though with frost. But it was nothing of the kind. God had spread a table for them in the wilderness. They called the mysterious food "manna." It was all about them, well within the reach of all, of easy access to young and old, bread from heaven, sweet to the taste, satisfying to their needs. It could be baked or boiled. The rabbis had a tradition that said it tasted like whatever kind of food a person desired. It would melt in the mouth.

Thus God meets our spiritual hunger. He showers upon us all that there is in Christ and in His Word to satisfy our hungry souls.

Take the Word of God, for instance. We need only reach out our hands and take it, 773,692 divinely inspired words (592,439 in the Old Testament and 181,253 in the New), and each and every word is God-breathed. What an inexhaustible provision for our daily spiritual needs. Christ too! He is the true Bread from heaven, manna enough and to spare for our hungry souls.

But then came *the disobedience of the people.* The rules for gathering the manna were simple, and they were intended as a test of obedience. There were three rules. First there was the *simple* rule. The manna came down with the dew and vanished with the sun. The person too lazy to gather his or her daily supply went hungry. There was nothing else.

It could not be stored. A person could not gather enough on Monday to last all week. It perished if an attempt was made to hoard it. Similarly, we must feast on the Word day by day. And we must be up before the sun waxes hot, that is, before the rush and bustle of our busy lives rob us of our time for gathering our daily bread.

There was also the *Sabbath* rule. No manna came on the Sabbath, God's day of rest; but a double portion came the day before, and stayed fresh. The principle of rest is essential to life. Even planets have periods of growth and periods of rest.

Finally, there was the *special* rule. A pot of manna was miraculously preserved in the tabernacle, generation after generation, to remind us that God will feed us until we want no more.

Devotion 29

Solomon's Three Books

Proverbs

Proverbs 2:12, 16

The queen of Sheba came from distant shores to sit at Solomon's feet. Across the dreary dunes of the desert, up the long reaches of the Nile, and on into the hill country of Judah she came, there to drink deep of the wise man's wonderful words. The fame of Solomon's wisdom was heralded far and wide, but his wisdom was not for his generation alone. Solomon was inspired of God to write it down. Under the guidance of the Holy Spirit, Solomon reduced his insights regarding government, psychology, and natural history into homespun proverbs, witty sayings that capsulize truth and make it easy to remember.

The sacred historian tells us that Solomon wrote three thousand proverbs (I Kings 4:32), of which only about a third have survived. Some take the pithy proverbs of the book of Proverbs to be promises as, for instance, the one that says: "Train up a child in the way he should go: and when he is old, he will not depart from it" (22:6). But that and similar proverbs are not unconditional *promises*; they state *principles*. And that is what the proverbs of Solomon are: principles to live by.

The book of Proverbs falls into three sections. The first nine chapters deal with *moral* issues. Solomon personifies wisdom as a woman, standing at life's crossroads, pleading with those who pass by to come and sample her wares. He contrasts this pure and lovely woman with the adulteress and harlot. In one of his graphic pictorial passages, Solomon tells how he watched from his window as a woman of the world won a youthful wanderer to her lusts. It is a sad commentary on Solomon's own moral torpidity that he made no attempt to warn the lad or to stop the woman. He should have put her to death. He seems to have been well versed in her persuasive powers. At least he tells us just what she said. His attitude, as he watched the drama unfold beneath his eyes, seems to have been one of detached philosophical interest. It was just another entry in his case book (Prov. 7:6–27).

In the next nine or ten chapters, Solomon deals with *miscellaneous* issues, comparing and contrasting the lifestyles of the godly person on the one hand and the godless on the other. "Fools make a mock at sin," he says (14:9). "There is a way that seemeth right unto a man," he says, "but the end thereof are the ways of death" (16:25). We recognize scores of such sayings.

The rest of the book deals with *monarchical* issues, advice given to those who are in authority. "Take away the wicked from before the king, and his throne shall be established in righteousness," he says (25:5). "When the wicked are multiplied, transgression increaseth" (29:16). We see these deathless principles at work in our own land.

The trouble with Solomon was that he never took his own advice. What he *was* spoke so loudly that his son, Rehoboam, never listened to a word he said. Who was the greater fool, Solomon or his son?

We can be grateful that Jesus said, "A greater than Solomon is here" (Matt. 12:42). He Himself was wisdom incarnate—and He practiced what He preached.

Devotion 30

Solomon's Three Books

Ecclesiastes

Solomon wrote one book when he was young, a book of *romance*; a second book in his middle age, a book of *rules*; and a final book when he was old, a book of *regrets*. That last book we call Ecclesiastes. In it Solomon reflects on the course and consequences of a misspent life. He addresses it to young people, doubtless in the hope that they will not repeat his own follies.

God had visited Solomon on two occasions and loaded him with blessings and benefits. He visited him a third time in wrath. It was not so much his lustful lifestyle, for Solomon was able to more or less legalize his lust by marrying the women he wanted. It was his toleration for the foul and fierce pagan gods of his wives and his actual worship of them that brought down God's wrath upon his head.

Stunned, Solomon pondered his follies and then took up his pen. The text for his long sermon was doubtless taken from Psalm 39. His topic was the vanity of life "under the sun"—the vanity, emptiness and folly of living as though there were no end to life, no God in heaven, and no world but this one. The book is a sermon based on Solomon's experiences as a backslider, his belated repentance, and his inadequate conclusions about life. "Vanity" can be written across a life lived without God, a life dominated by the things of time and sense. Roughly paraphrased, the word *vanity* can be rendered "chasing the wind."

Solomon tells us of some of the things he had *sought*. He drew on a wide experience of life because he had gone in for everything "under the sun." To begin with, he had tried the world of *thought*. Surely the answer to life was to become an intellectual and have people come to you to drink in your wisdom. When he achieved success and fame along this line, it left him unsatisfied. Next, he tried the world of *thrills* and abandoned himself to pleasure. He sought to gratify the flesh and enjoy the world. Satiated with pleasure, he gave up that pursuit as being insane.

Finally, he tried the world of *things* and sought joy in making money. Soon he had everything money could buy, but nothing satisfied and he actually ended up contemplating suicide. "I hated life," he said.

Next, Solomon tells us of the things he had *seen*. Everywhere he looked it was the same sad story—nothing satisfied. He had been living for time and for the things of time. He belatedly discovered that God has "set the world (eternity) in the heart" (3:11). Solomon was like the modern corporate executive who had reached the top of the ladder only to discover it was up against the wrong wall.

Finally, Solomon tells us of the things he had *studied*. He became increasingly cynical, especially about women. And no wonder! His palace must have been a pandemonium of jealousy, spite, and intrigue, thanks to the thousand women he kept in his harem.

Worse still, Solomon was haunted by the fear of death. He mentions it more and more. He dreaded death and hated growing old.

In the last two chapters, Solomon finally emerged from the fog and began to look beyond and above the sun. And there was God! God hadn't moved! *He,* Solomon, was the one who had moved. Now he had to come back to God to face judgment for his misspent life. It was a frightening thought.

In the end, he wrote his book. The Holy Spirit enabled him to do so and gave him this last chance to make amends. And so, no doubt, he has, for people have been reading his warnings in Ecclesiastes for nearly three thousand years. And surely many have been warned.

Devotion 31

Solomon's Three Books

Song of Solomon—Part 1

Song of Solomon 7:10

It is not at all surprising that Solomon became the author of three of the most enduring books in the world. The books reflect different states in his remarkable career. One book records his great *disappointment,* the inevitable result of his own lustful lifestyle. The second book illustrates his great *discernment,* the genius he had for reducing great truths to simple sayings. The final book demonstrates the great *disparity* so sadly evident between what he taught and what he wrought.

First, we consider the Song of Solomon. This is a *book of romance.* It is a love song, one in which Solomon was inspired by the Holy Spirit to tell us about the one woman he could not have. She turned him down, despite all his efforts to turn her thoughts and desires to him.

It is often claimed that in the Song of Solomon, Solomon is a type of Christ. How can that be? He is a type of Christ in respect to the *kingdom,* for when Christ comes back, He will reign as David, putting down all His foes; and then He will reign as Solomon, in prosperity, peace, and power. Solomon's personal life, however, was a national scandal. He came very close to apostasy and did more than any other king to undermine and eventually destroy the kingdom of Israel. Look, for instance, at Solomon's proposal to the Shulamite! "I have sixty wives," he said, "and another eighty women I am living with. Indeed, I have more women that I can count, but you can be first" (see 6:8). Who can put such words into the mouth of the pure and holy Jesus?

There is *another,* however, who plays out his part in this song of songs, a beloved shepherd to whom the Shulamite has already given her heart. Solomon exerts all his personal charm, his way with words, his position, his power, and his ability to gratify desires for worldly success in order to awe and win the Shulamite. If Solomon is a type of anyone in this book, it is the prince of this world, who would seduce us from Christ as Solomon tried to turn away the Shulamite's affections from her beloved shepherd to himself. Indeed, this is the real key to the book.

Though abducted by Solomon to his pavilion, and though courted ardently by Solomon, and though exposed to the urgings of Solomon's other women, women who had surrendered to his personality, promises, and passion, the Shulamite remained true to her absent beloved.

Her final rejection of Solomon's overtures is classic, and it gives us the key to overcoming temptation. "I am my beloved's," she said, "and his desire is toward me" (7:10). Note that! She did not say "my desire is toward him" (though, of course, that was perfectly true), but "his desire is toward me." Solomon had no more to say.

Surely, that should be our stand in temptation's hour. "I am my Beloved's, and *His* desire is toward *me*." Think of it! The desire of the Lord Himself, the King of glory, Creator of the universe, the One whom angels worship, is toward *me*! Wonder of wonders! Surely no temptation can be successful in the face of the wonder of that. It is only when we forget this marvelous truth that temptation has its way.

Devotion 32

Solomon's Three Books

Song of Solomon—Part 2

Song of Solomon 5:10–16

The Song of Solomon begins with an hour of trouble. The Shulamite, having been abducted into Solomon's pavilion in the country, finds herself virtually a prisoner. She calls out to her absent shepherd. She longs for his love. She delights to speak his name. The daughters of Jerusalem, who love the lustful Solomon, overhear her and alarm her.

Then Solomon comes. He flatters her and makes all kinds of promises to her, offering her silver and gold in exchange for her love. Then he hurries off to a banquet, satisfied he has made a good impression, one he can exploit at a later date.

But he is mistaken. The Shulamite's beloved shepherd comes to where she is, confined in Solomon's country pavilion, and she and her shepherd exchange endearments. She describes his desired rustic table and contrasts it with Solomon's loaded board.

This hour of tenderness ends, and the court women reappear. They try to stir up the Shulamite's passion, hoping it can be used to snare her. Their goal is to detach her affections from her shepherd and to seduce her into making an alliance with the worldly prince Solomon. They do not succeed. She sharply rebukes them and tells them not to incite her desires. She gives them her testimony. She tells how once she thought that she had lost her beloved. Though it was nighttime, she had gone to look for him, only to be frightened by the night watchmen. Thankfully, however, she found her shepherd. "I held him," she says, "and would not let him go" (3:4).

Solomon, tiring of the country, now decides to return to Jerusalem. He approaches the city, carrying along the Shulamite in a closed carriage. The way is lined by his admiring subjects. They make comments about him. They praise his worldly passions, his power, his possessions, and his exalted position. They comment on the spectacle of the impressive imperial guard marching beside the king. They talk about his marriage to the queen and recall how he had been crowned by his mother on that occasion.

Although she is now a prisoner, the Shulamite manages to arrange another meeting with her shepherd. He says to her, "Thou art fair, my love" (4:1). She tells him that all that she has is his.

Solomon's court women reappear, and the Shulamite tells them of a dream she once had. In her dream her beloved came, but she had been too lazy to respond, so he had gone away. She had run after him, only to find herself again in trouble with the watchmen. Thankfully, it was only a dream. She describes to the women the beauty of her beloved, and they want to know how *they* can find him. Suddenly suspicious of their motives, she refuses to tell them.

Now Solomon comes back, armed with flatteries. His words are distressingly frank and brazen. His description of her charms are daring and distressful. The Shulamite, however, is arrayed in the armor of her goodness, and he does not dare to touch her, powerful as he is. Through it all, she remains true to her beloved. "I am my beloved's," she said, "and his desire is toward me" (7:10). Solomon, silenced and defeated, lets her go. He fails to achieve his goal of winning her away from her shepherd.

The book ends with two last requests. The shepherd pleads with his beloved Shulamite to let him hear her voice. The Shulamite pleads with the shepherd to come soon and receive her unto himself.

When viewed thus, the Song of Solomon teaches us how to overcome the wiles of the prince of this world and how to be victorious and true to our Beloved when exposed to the snares of this world.

Devotion 33

JESUS AND HIS BIBLE

ISAIAH 53:1

The first glimpse we get of Jesus, between His birth and His baptism, He is in His rightful place, right at the heart of things. He is in the midst of the doctors, the famous rabbis to whose schools rich men sent their sons. He is there, listening to them and asking them questions. He makes no attempt to teach them, for at the age of twelve, that would have been considered presumptuous. But a wise person knows how to direct and develop people's thoughts by asking them appropriate and challenging questions.

Doubtless these rabbis were wrapped up in the so-called "oral law." According to the rabbis this oral law was given by Moses to supplement the written Law. The custodians of this fictitious "oral law" kept adding to it. It did not contain divine truth in all its pristine purity but rather the teachings and the traditions of men. By the time of the Middle Ages, it had grown to the size of the *Encyclopedia Britannica* and was carried in the capacious minds and memories of a handful of prodigies. Already in Jesus' day, this so-called oral law was given precedence over the written Word of God and was on the way to becoming what we now call the Talmud. It was already replacing the Torah as the final authority in matters of faith and morals.

So, we can well imagine what kind of questions Jesus posed to these rabbis—"What think ye of Christ, whose Son is He?"; "Of whom does Isaiah 53 speak, of the prophet or of some other man?"; "If David, in the Spirit, in Psalm 110 called the Messiah 'Lord,' how is He then His Son?"

By the time He was thirty years of age, Jesus knew His Bible in Hebrew and Greek as no man before or since. No doubt He had memorized it and, along with it, all the teachings and traditions that fenced it in.

Isaiah 53 begins with *the Lord and His Bible.* The prophet begins with a sigh: "Who hath believed our report?" he asks. Practically nobody! For, as Jesus once declared, "A prophet is not without honour, save in his own country, and in his own house" (Matt. 13:57).

By the time Isaiah wrote chapter 53 of his book, he was getting used to being ignored. For instance, he had foretold the coming Assyrian invasion and had been ignored. His prophecies had been fulfilled, however, for where once the great cities of Israel had stood, now the lion roared and the jackal roamed. He warned next of the coming Babylonian invasion—and was ignored. Now, in this matchless chapter, he told of a coming, suffering Messiah. Again, he was ignored.

Well, there was one Man who read Isaiah 53 with unswerving belief—Jesus! "Who hath believed our report?" cried Isaiah. Jesus believed it! He believed every word of it. To Him every word was inerrant, inspired, God-breathed. And the whole chapter speaks of Him.

We can picture the Lord Jesus soaking up the Scriptures at His mother's knee and then at the feet of the local rabbi in the Nazareth synagogue. Soon He was to be seen studying the Scriptures on His own. He would ponder its passages even as He pounded nails into a board in the workshop at Nazareth. He based His whole life on God's Word. When He came to live in this world, He could say, "Lo, I come (in the volume of the book it is written of me,) to do thy will, O God" (Heb. 10:7; cf. Ps. 40:7). Every move He made was in keeping with that Word.

"Yes! Isaiah," He would say, pausing at each verse, each phrase, each clause of Isaiah 53, "I believe that. That is written of Me. That's Me! I am going to experience that, suffer that, fulfill that. Who believes you? I do. And it is going to cost Me My life."

Devotion 34

A Man of Sorrows, Acquainted with Grief

Isaiah 53:3

He is despised and rejected of men," says the prophet, "a man of sorrows, and acquainted with grief." The expression "man of sorrows" can be translated "man of pains." We would have found it easier to accept had Isaiah called Him "a man of war," or "a man of God," or "a man of might and miracle." But

"Man of sorrows," what a name
For the Son of God Who came
Ruined sinners to reclaim!
Hallelujah! What a Savior![1]

Surely, if ever there was a man on earth who should have been exempt from suffering and pain, it was Jesus. But no! He was "a man of pain."

Not far from where I was born and brought up, there stands, on the bank of the river Wye, the stark but impressive ruins of an abbey. It has a history running back some seven or eight hundred years. It was founded and built by an agrarian order of monks and, like so many other abbeys in England, it grew to be rich and powerful. In time, indeed, the abbeys rivaled the very throne.

Henry VIII decided to put an end to all that. The vast holdings of the abbeys he gave to his favorites at court. The lead from the roofs of the abbeys was torn off, melted down, and sold to enrich the king. The wind and the weather did the rest. All that remains of Tintern Abbey today is the walled skeleton of an impressive ruin. No one visiting the abbey would imagine for a moment that it was designed to be

---

1. Philip P. Bliss, "Hallelujah! What a Savior!" 1875.

the ruin it now is. On the contrary, it was *designed* to be a magnificent building. It was never intended to be treated the way it was.

We live in a ruined world, a world of suffering, sorrow, and death. But it was not designed that way. Tintern Abbey was designed to last almost forever; even its ruins bear witness to that. The ruined abbey presents us today with a mixture of order and chaos, just as the world in which we live presents us with a mixture of order and chaos, of good and evil.

It was to deal with the ruin that Jesus came into the world. He did not come as a tourist to shake His head and mourn over the vast devastation done to His own handiwork. He came to deal with it. And that meant becoming involved. It meant becoming a man of sorrows, acquainted with grief. So Isaiah takes us to the cross.

Some time ago I read a book written by a man who went through the horrors of Auschwitz. He was a child when he was torn away from his home, loaded onto a boxcar, and shipped across endless miles of misery to a place where torture and torment was the sum and substance of life. His mother and his little sister were murdered, and their bodies burned. A smudge of smoke was the last he saw of them. He survived. He was always hungry, always terrified, but he survived.

God died in this tormented prisoner's soul on the day he witnessed the hanging of a young boy. The commandant read the indictment, but all eyes were on the boy. He was hanged for stealing a potato, and the inmates of the camp were forced to march past his gallows. The worst part of it was he was so light it took him a long time to die. The survivor collapsed into ruins himself that day. He heard someone in the ranks say, "Where is God *now*?" He said to himself, "God is dead." He added, "That night the soup tasted of corpses."

But God was not dead and is not dead. The answer to the bitter question, "Where is God now?" is simple. He is in the same place He was when His Son was hanged. For Jesus came to get involved. He became a man of sorrows, acquainted with grief. The answer to the problem of suffering, pain, and death in the world is bound up with the suffering, pain, and death of Jesus and with His glorious resurrection, ascension, and certain return.

Devotion 35

By His Stripes We Are Healed

Isaiah 53:5

The healing of the body is part of the tidal wave of blessing that comes to us by way of the cross. Our resurrection bodies will be immune to sin and suffering. They will be like Christ's glorious body, beyond the reach of disease, disaster, death, and decay.

When He lived on earth, the Lord healed everyone who came His way. He never lost a case. He never charged a fee.

Can you imagine Jesus behaving like some modern "healers" do? Imagine Him saying: "Peter, you go on ahead into the city and rent the auditorium. Book it for seven nights. Matthew, you get some posters made: 'Famous Nazareth Healer in town for seven incredible nights.' Thomas, you take charge of the stage effects. Put up some crutches and display some testimonials. Nathanael, you take care of the healing line. Be sure to weed out the hard cases—and don't forget the hand signals we've agreed on. Andrew, you be in charge of catching those I knock over backward. Judas, you be in charge of the offerings. We're really going to cash in this week." Why the very thought is contrary to everything we know of the Lord Jesus. Never in our wildest dreams could we imagine Him acting in any such way.

How did He do it then? Well, on one occasion He went to a local sanatorium (the Pool of Bethesda) and picked out the most hopeless case, a man who had suffered for thirty-eight years. He healed *him*. On another occasion He cleaned up a small leper colony, healing all ten of the lepers at once. He broke up every funeral He ever attended by raising the dead—even a man who had been dead for days. The blind, the lame, the deaf, the dumb, the palsied, the leprous, the demon possessed, the dead!—there was no case too hard for Him. *That* was the kind of healing that was wrought by His *life*, the healing of the body. Dr. Luke records an occasion when the Lord was surrounded by "a great multitude of people" who "came to hear him, and to be healed of their diseases." He "healed them all," Luke says (6:17–19). Matthew records a similar healing session and says that the healing Jesus gave so fully and freely fulfilled the prophecy of Isaiah 53:4 (Matt. 8:17).

The healing He brought by His *death,* the healing that has continued on a global scale, from that day to this, is the healing of the soul. As the hymn puts it,

> There's not a friend like the lowly Jesus,
> No, not one! no, not one!
> None else can heal all our souls' diseases,
> No, not one! no, not one![1]

The Lord's healing of both body and soul (the healing of people's bodies during His life, and the healing of our souls by His death) does not exhaust Isaiah's words. The ultimate healing will take place at the rapture. In I Corinthians 15 we have a revelation of what our resurrection bodies will be like. They will forever defy the law of sin and death. We will be glorified and our bodies will be just like the resurrection body of Jesus. In our resurrection bodies we shall live on and on, forever and ever, in a tumult of bliss and full of that "joy unspeakable and full of glory" of which the Bible speaks (I Peter 1:8).

Well, Isaiah, what do you think of that? You will share in it too! You, too, will come bounding out of your grave, shouting along with us: "O death, where is thy sting? O grave, where is thy victory?" (I Cor. 15:55).

1. Johnson Oatman Jr., "No, Not One!" 1895.

Devotion 36

Obadiah

Obadiah's book is little more than a mere pamphlet. Indeed, it contains less than two dozen verses. It is, in fact, a tale of two cities, Petra and Jerusalem. It is also the story of two peoples, the Edomites and the Jews. Moreover, it is the story of twins, Esau and Jacob—unidentical twins, different in appearance, different in appetite, different in appeal. The one boy, Esau, appealed to his father. The other boy, Jacob, appealed to his mother. The one boy was a killer, a wild man, a professional hunter. The other boy was a keeper, one who had a heart for the flock.

From these two boys came two nations. The nation of Edom, which descended from Esau, was wild, godless, and proud, living on the plunder of caravans and wayfarers. The other nation, Israel, descended from Jacob, was a chosen nation, raised up by God to be a testimony to all others. There was a long history of war and strife between these two peoples. Had the Edomites held out a helping hand to the Hebrews as they traveled from Egypt to Canaan, the story might have been a different one. The Edomites might have found shelter beneath the wings of Jehovah. Instead, they chose rather to hinder and oppose. In the end they produced a man called Herod the Great, the monster of a man who tried to murder the infant Christ of God in His bed.

The most spectacular city of Edom was the rock city of Petra. It was surrounded by a wild, untamed terrain, a tangle of mountains, deep canyons, and rock shelves with strips of fertile land here and there. Here was the haunt of the sliding serpent, the stinging scorpion, and the soaring eagle. The Edomites thought their country to be impregnable and boasted of their place in the sun.

When Nebuchadnezzar invaded Jerusalem, the Edomites were thrilled. They became his willing aides, following in the wake of the Babylonian conquerors, urging them on, cheering their triumphs, helping them round up fleeing Jews. When Jerusalem fell, they cheered and fell on the spoil. Moreover, they took an active part in sacking the city, in catching fleeing Jews, and in seizing their land.

No wonder Obadiah spoke out: "Though thou exalt thyself as the eagle, and though thou set thy nest among the stars, thence will I bring thee down, saith the LORD" (v. 4). "Thou shalt be cut off for ever" (v. 10). And so it came to be. The rock city of Petra is now just a place for tourists to go.

As for that other city, Jerusalem, the prophet had a word for her too. Ruin for Petra! Restoration for Judah! And that, too, has come to be. Yea, and beyond the turmoil of today, in the coming day of the Lord, the prophet saw a triumphant Zion. He saw the banners of the Christ unfurled and the nations trooping to Jerusalem proclaiming holiness to the Lord (v. 17).

Obadiah teaches us that God is ever on the throne. In the end, He always settles accounts with those who attack His own. More, God does not allow a temporary lapse by His people, however sad and serious it may be, to turn Him from His goals—whether for Israel or for His church.

Devotion 37

JONAH

Down! Down! Down! Thus the Holy Spirit describes Jonah's early steps in his life of disobedience. Moreover, it was not until he touched bottom that this Old Testament prodigal came to himself.

First, we have *the word from God.* "The word of the LORD came unto Jonah" (1:1). Jonah had no doubt as to either the source or the substance of the word that came to him: "Arise, go to Nineveh, that great city, and cry against it; for their wickedness is come up before me" (v. 2). What galled Jonah was the knowledge that, if he did as he was told, Nineveh might repent. And if Nineveh repented, then God would change His mind; and Nineveh would be spared—to become the very rod of God to thrash guilty Israel. Jonah decided that Nineveh was the last place he intended to go.

So he took off for Tarshish, to what in those days was "the uttermost part of the earth." "Yet forty days, and Nineveh shall be overthrown" (3:4). That was the message. Well, it would take God more than forty days to catch up to him!

Then came *the word with God.* For God had both the wind and the fish waiting for this willful prophet. He would give this wayward witness of His a taste of that hell to which he was all too ready to consign the Ninevites. Indeed, that is just where Jonah eventually confessed himself to be—in "the belly of hell" (2:2). He endured his terrors for three days and three nights before he was willing to go to Nineveh. God had no thought of changing His mind. So, finally, Jonah prayed. Oh, how he prayed! Verse after verse of the Psalms came to mind. He strung them together in a string of pleas for help. And God heard and answered, and the word came to him again: "Yet forty days, and Nineveh shall be overthrown." Jonah discovered that the sandglass of forty days was set to run, not from the time he received the message, but from the time Nineveh did.

So comes *the word for God.* Jonah went to Nineveh and, arriving at its gate, he must have been a ghastly sight. The gastric juices of the fish had doubtless done their deadly work. He looked like a living corpse. He began to preach. His prophecy contained only eight words: "Yet forty days, and Nineveh shall be overthrown," but Jonah preached them with authority and power. He himself was the real message, a living epistle to be known and read by all people. The terrified Ninevites looked at Jonah, listened to Jonah, and repented to the last man, woman, and child.

And Jonah sulked. He sat in his shanty at a spot where he could see the fires fall. And nothing happened. He was enraged. He complained bitterly to God. And God stooped down to reason with him. The last we see of Jonah, he was still sulking, still mad, like the elder brother of the Lord's parable (Luke 15:25–32). But, in the end, Jonah too repented. He went home and wrote his book, and God put it in the Bible. And Jonah has rejoiced ever since, with joy unspeakable and full of glory, as people in all ages and in many lands have read his book and been saved, or studied it and responded to the call to proclaim God's Word in all parts of the world.

Devotion 38

Haggai

Haggai was a very old man. As a boy he had been hauled off to Babylon as a slave. Behind him lay the smoking ruins of Jerusalem and the temple. Alongside him tramped the surviving remnant of the chosen people of God.

At length the boy captive saw the city itself, great Babylon, which sat astride the Euphrates and ruled the world. It was to be his home from boyhood to old age. But he would never forget his roots. He would recall a thousand times the promises of Jeremiah and the preaching of Ezekiel. The startling visions of Daniel also would come to mind, visions that ran down the avenues of time to distant ages yet unborn.

His generation grew up, and another took its place. Haggai could not help but notice that this new generation had little longing left for the Land of Promise. Indeed, when Cyrus issued his famous decree, emancipating the Jewish captives he had inherited from the Babylonians, most Jews weren't interested at all. They had been born in Babylon. They had made it their home. The vast Persian Empire, covering some two million square miles, was their emporium. It was a great place to do business and grow rich. Of the twenty-four orders of priests, only four took Cyrus seriously. Of the entire Levitical tribe, only seventy-four responded. The treasures and pleasures of Babylon had most of the Jews in their grip.

Haggai, however, responded with joy. He was going home! And, at first, his hopes burned high, for when they arrived back in Jerusalem an altar was built and the foundations of a new temple were laid. But then it all fizzled out, and Haggai was outraged. The Spirit of God fell upon him, and He began to preach.

"Consider your ways," he cried (1:5). They were eating and drinking, buying and building, plowing and planting—and God blew on it, and it all came to nothing. Why? Because *God's* house was being neglected—that was why.

When, under the lash and spur of Haggai, the people finally stirred themselves and completed the house, another problem surfaced. The old men wept because they remembered the glittering, golden splendor of Solomon's temple, and this new temple was a mere ghost of a temple compared with that one. They wept. "Never mind!" God said, "This house will be blessed in a way never known by Solomon's temple. *God Himself* will visit *this* temple." And so it was that when Jesus came, He did indeed visit that temple. He visited it as a *Babe* in Mary's arms, as a *Boy* full grown, and as a *Man,* with whip in hand and with fire in His eye, He came to cast out and cleanse. Solomon's golden shrine had watched in vain for such a visitation of God manifest in flesh.

The bottom line, as we would say, in Haggai's prophecy was simply this—if we put God's house first, God will put our house first.

Devotion 39

ZECHARIAH

Haggai and Zechariah were contemporaries. Haggai was an old man; Zechariah was a young one. The Lord referred to Zechariah in his denunciation of Jerusalem: "Ye serpents, ye generation of vipers, how can ye escape the damnation of hell? . . . upon you [shall] come all the righteous blood shed upon the earth, from the blood of righteous Abel unto the blood of Zacharias son of Barachias, whom ye slew between the temple and the altar" (Matt. 23:33, 35). Abel was the first martyr in the Old Testament, and the prophet Zechariah was the last.

The temple had been finished, thanks to the spur and lash of old Haggai. But the "Canaanites," that is, wicked, unbelieving Jews (Zech. 14:21), were now in the house of the Lord, and Zechariah was outraged. At first, his prophecies took an apocalyptic turn. He looked far down the distant ages and his preaching was far beyond the grasp of his hearers.

"I see a red horse!" he cried. "Now I see four horns and four carpenters." He might as well have been speaking a foreign language. "I see a man measuring the city! I can see the high priest in filthy raiment! Now I see a Branch, now two olive trees. Now I see a woman sitting in a container. Now come two women with wide wings like a stork. They are carrying the woman to Babylon. Now I see four chariots and multicolored horses going off in all directions. And now, mark this well, I see the *high priest* being crowned like a king."

We can well imagine Zechariah's hearers making no sense at all of all that. Indeed, to this very day, multitudes in the church still cannot decode the apocalyptic message Zechariah gave. We can imagine that the Jews were increasingly annoyed with the prophet for setting forth truth they simply could not grasp, not that they liked him any better when he put aside his riddles and spoke in plain language.

He foretold both the coming Greek and Roman invasions, and both the first and second comings of Christ. He saw Jesus riding in triumph into Jerusalem—on a donkey of all things. He saw the coming of the

Antichrist. He saw Christ being sold for a handful of silver, and the money being used to buy a potter's field. He saw God's sword awakened, the Shepherd smitten, the sheep scattered. Yes, and he saw, too, the glorious return of Christ, splitting Olivet asunder, and all nations beating a path to His feet. He saw a day when there would be no more unbelievers in the house of the Lord.

Then, one morning, Zechariah took his usual walk around the temple. Some Jews saw him coming. "Behold this dreamer cometh," they said. "Let us kill him and put an end to his sermons and signs." And so they did, accursed "Canaanites" that they were.

Well, they got rid of the prophet, but they couldn't get rid of his book. The Spirit of God saw to it that it was added to the Bible itself—its closing verses anticipating the day when "holiness unto the Lord" would be engraved on every pot and pan in Jerusalem and all men would know that holiness is what it's all about.

Devotion 40

Malachi

Malachi was the John the Baptist of the Old Testament—the voice of one crying in the wilderness. He was also like the Lord's disciple, John. When John took his pen to write the last book of the New Testament, everyone else was dead. His brother, James, was dead. Old "camel knees," James, the Lord's brother, was dead. Peter and Paul had been dead for thirty to thirty-five years. It was the same with Malachi in the Old Testament. When Malachi took his pen to write the last book of the Old Testament, everyone else was dead—Zerubbabel, Joshua, Haggai, Zechariah, Ezra, and Nehemiah—all were gone.

To be a prophet of God had always been a lonely business. It must have seemed to Malachi that he was very much alone indeed. The fatal tide of current events had set toward the flood. It was coming in strongly now, and the trend was away from the *Torah,* away from the Bible, and toward the *Talmud* and the traditions and teachings of men. By the time of Christ, the Jewish world would be firmly controlled by rabbinical Judaism, by Pharasaical hypocrisy, by legalism, and by Sadducean liberalism. It would prove to be a deadly brew against truth incarnate in Christ.

Although Malachi did not date his prophecy, we can arrive at a very possible date. The clue is found in Daniel's famous prophecy of the seventy weeks in Daniel 9. From a given date (which turned out to be the date when Artaxerxes signed the decree that permitted Nehemiah to go to Jerusalem and rebuild its walls), three prophetic events were to be dated. *One* had to do with the murder of the Messiah—He was to be "cut off" after sixty-nine "weeks" (of years) had passed—that is, after 483 years. *Another* had to do with the Lord's second coming. It focused on one "week" of years—the seven-year period dominated by the coming Antichrist. The *third* prophesied event was to take place seven "weeks" (i.e., forty-nine years) after the decree of Artaxerxes was signed. The date brings us down to the year 396 B.C. What was so significant about this date? As to that, God remains *silent,* and that is the whole point of it. After that date, God would remain silent. That was the time when Malachi preached. After that, God remained silent for four hundred years, the period covered by the events long since recorded in Daniel 11.

What did this last prophet have to say? He said that toward their sovereign Maker, the people adopted *a contradictory attitude,* arguing with God. Toward their salvation message, they had adopted *a contemptuous attitude,* offering their leftovers to God. Toward their separated ministers (the Levites), they had adopted *a corrupting attitude.* Toward the sanctity of marriage, they had adopted *a callous attitude*—by the time of Christ, a man could divorce his wife for burning his food. Toward the sinful majority, they had adopted *a complaisant attitude.* Toward their secular materialism, they had adopted *a carnal attitude,* robbing God without compunction or hesitation. And toward their sacred manuscripts, they had adopted a *careless attitude.* No wonder Malachi preached!

Malachi ends on a disturbing note, even more disturbing for the Jews since the Old Testament came to an end along with his prophecy. Thus both the book of Malachi and the Old Testament end with the sobering word "curse"! The Jews did not like it at all, so they regrouped the books, putting Malachi elsewhere and ending with Chronicles instead. That did not help them avoid the curse. However, God overruled their action. The long list of names with which 1 Chronicles begins dovetails right into the list of names with which Matthew begins—a list of names that takes us straight to Jesus! So God began all over again. The Old Testament ends with a *curse;* the New Testament begins with a *cradle.* God began to speak again but this time not through mere people alone. This time He spoke through His Son—"the Word made flesh."

Devotion 41

Walking on the Waves

MATTHEW 14:22–33

He had never done it before. He would never do it again. But for one glorious, dizzy moment, Peter walked upon the waves. And they felt solid as cement, even while they moved like a roller coaster beneath his feet. If he didn't look at them, he was all right. It took him a moment to get his balance and get the hang of how to walk on a moving platform, but he did it. And thereon hangs a tale. We really have three pictures to examine here.

First, there is a picture of *peril.* It had been a most remarkable day of sublime teaching, teaching that touched the heart and stirred the soul. But secretly everyone had hoped for a miracle—just one would do for now! And what a miracle it was when it came! There was the Lord, and there was the lad, and there were the loaves, a small boy's little lunch, magnanimously given to the Master. And suddenly there was bread enough and to spare to feed upwards of ten thousand hungry people! No wonder everyone wanted to crown Him king then and there! The Lord, however, quickly defused that package of high explosives. He sent the disciples away first because they were as excited as the rest. Then He stayed behind to quietly and efficiently dismiss the cheering multitudes.

"You fellows go on ahead. I'll meet you on the other side," He said. So off they went and, soon afterward, evening twilight faded; and the darkness came. What a position they were in—adrift on life's tempestuous sea, without Christ, and in the dark. Darkness was followed by danger. A storm came, and what a storm it was! The disciples, many of them old hands at sailing that lake, knew how dangerous a storm on Galilee could be. They were in peril, and they knew it.

But there was something they had forgotten. They were in the center of the Lord's will. His *intention put them* in that place of peril. His *intercession preserved them* in that place of peril. They were in the safest place on earth, in the very center of His will for them, right there, right then.

The next picture is one of *panic.* They were paralyzed with fear. The wind howled and the waves heaved, and the little ship was tossed about. Then they saw it, way out over the water: a human form climbing the crests of the wild waves and negotiating the deepest troughs. A ghost! After all, this was a demon-haunted lake. On its shores Christ had cast out many evil spirits. The disciples cried out in terror. Then came His cheerful hail: "It is I; be not afraid." Their terror fled. Jesus had come.

All this brings us to a picture of *Peter,* impulsive, impetuous Peter! Look at his *desire.* His desire was to walk upon those waves, to be like Jesus, to be with Jesus. Bravo, Simon Peter!

Notice also his *decision.* The Lord called to him to come. Peter flung his feet over the side and placed them on the nearest wave and let go! It was the bravest thing he ever did before Pentecost. Well done, Peter!

Note also his *despair.* One step, two steps. He could hardly believe it. Then, for a moment, distracted by the storm, he took his eyes off Jesus—and sank! *"Lord,"* he cried, *"save me."* It is the gospel in three words. And saved he was!

Come to think of it, that was the best thing that could have happened. Apart from that sudden despair, Peter might have boasted afterward about his experience. He might have started a cult. A defeat that leaves us humble is better than a victory that leaves us proud.

Devotion 42

Jesus Is Coming Again

Matthew 24:27–25:6

Four things about the second coming of Christ should fill our souls with joy.

First, *He is coming swiftly*: "As the lightning cometh out of the east, and shineth even unto the west; so shall the coming of the Son of man be" (Matt. 24:27). Once He steps into the sky, there will be no time to get right with God, no time to make amends. Swift as fast-paced lightning He will come. Lightning is incredibly swift. A spark from a cloud to the earth can measure as much as eight miles and can travel at the speed of 100 million feet per second. Lightning that reaches from cloud to cloud can be twenty to one hundred miles long. The Lord Jesus is coming at the speed of a lightning flash. It will be "in a moment," it will be "in the twinkling of an eye." It will be a happy moment for His own and a horrendous moment for His foes!

Lightning can be deadly. Sheet lightning has no particular form; it is just a bright flash in the sky, but forked lightning comes charged with millions of volts of electrical power. Jesus is coming like that, swiftly and in power.

Then, too, *He is coming solemnly*: "As in the days that were before the flood they were eating and drinking, marrying and giving in marriage, until . . . the flood came, and took them all away; so shall also the coming of the Son of man be" (Matt. 24:38–39). The years before the Flood were similar to the days in which we live. In Noah's day the true faith was rapidly disappearing and a pornographic society, one filled with violence, took its place. People were making tremendous strides in the fields of science, commerce, and the arts. Permissiveness was the popular attitude of a lawless society that allowed the guilty to go unpunished and endorsed all kinds of deviant behavior. The majority of people were ignorant of God's Word. They "knew not," Jesus said in His commentary on these things (Matt. 24:39). People were clever enough when it came to material things, but they were wholly blind to spiritual things. They ignored the signs that pointed to coming doom. They "knew not" until it was too late. So it was then. So it is today.

Then, too, *He is coming secretly*: "Watch therefore: for ye know not what hour your Lord doth come" (Matt. 24:42). This aspect of the Lord's second coming has to do with the *rapture,* not with the final return of the Lord to reign. The date of the final return will be known to those who believe. It will be exactly 1,260 days from the day the Antichrist seizes the rebuilt Jewish temple and begins the great tribulation to the day of Christ's return to reign (Rev. 12:6). Before that happens, the Lord is coming like a thief, coming secretly, when least expected, to snatch away His own people. "Of *that* day and that hour knoweth no man," Jesus said (Mark 13:32). In Matthew's account of this secret event, the Lord goes on to actually describe the rapture of the church (Matt. 24:36, 40–44). "Be ready!" That's the word!

Finally, like the bridegroom, *He is coming surely*: "Behold, the bridegroom cometh; go ye out to meet him," will be the cry (Matt. 25:6). Now we are invited to view the second coming from His point of view. A bridegroom—what a picture of eager anticipation! He has been gone for a long time, but He has been busy preparing a place for us, a home beyond the sky. His Spirit has been here in His stead, however, and has been busy calling out a people for His name. But one of these days, He will come. And we'll be gone! What a day of rejoicing that will be.

Devotion 43

He Is Risen

MATTHEW 28:6

Here are the salient facts:

1. A man who claimed to be God was crucified on a skull-shaped hill called Calvary. He was certified dead by the Roman centurion in charge. His death was accompanied by such awesome signs and wonders that His executioners owned Him to be the Son of God.
2. He was buried in a brand-new tomb, which was secured by a stone, a seal, and a detachment of soldiers. These precautions were taken by the authorities to ensure that nobody tampered with the tomb.
3. Three days later the tomb was empty. The stone was rolled back, and the guards fled in terror. A visitor from another world proclaimed Him to be alive.
4. All through that day, and on into the weeks ahead, people saw Him alive.

Such are the facts. Either they are gloriously true, or else they are a collection of fables and fantasies.

Here are the arguments of those who deny the resurrection:

The first rumor to be circulated was that the disciples had stolen the body. To support this falsehood the Jewish Sanhedrin paid the soldiers who had reported the resurrection, "large money" (Matt. 28:12) to say that, while they slept, the disciples came and stole the body. This was obviously a lie. For one thing, the penalty in the Roman army for sleeping on guard was death. If it had been true, that they had been asleep, the soldiers would have been the first to deny it. The Jewish authorities assured them. "We can bribe the governor," they said. "You don't have to worry."

But what a sorry lie it was! Imagine someone coming into a court of law and saying to the judge and jury: "Your Honor, and members of the jury, I consider myself a competent witness because when the events I have described happened, I was sound asleep!"

The second theory is that Christ did not really die. It is claimed He swooned on the cross and was hastily buried, but revived in the cool of the tomb and managed to free Himself from His grave clothes. He then escaped into the night and three days later showed Himself alive—thus giving rise to fables about His resurrection.

This view raises a multitude of problems. It assumes that a Roman soldier mistook a swooning man for a dead man. It assumes that the Lord's friends embalmed a living man when, surely, they of all people would have noticed had He still been alive. It assumes, moreover, that the Lord's bitter enemies, who had moved heaven and earth to get Him crucified, would leave the scene of execution before making sure He was dead. The records declare, however, that the centurion took no chances. He ordered a soldier to stab Jesus in the side with a spear to make quite sure He was dead.

Jesus recovered and escaped, says this view. But, every bone in His body was out of joint; and He was fearfully wounded in both His hands and feet. Yet, according to this theory, He first unwound the grave clothes that bound Him, then rewound them, to give the impression that He had risen through them. He pushed back the heavy, sealed stone that barred His escape and eluded the guard. Then, contrary to all we know of His peerless character, He perpetrated a lie by pretending to have come back from the dead. This view makes no sense. It generates more problems than it solves.

The third view is that the disciples saw a ghost. He Himself, however, effectively put an end to *that* view when He entered the upper room in His resurrection body and not only ate a meal but also invited those present to handle Him.

Years ago a German pastor known for his faith was sneered at by a speaker at a giant rally of the Nazis in Berlin. "Pastor Schutez," said the speaker, "you are a fool. Fancy believing in a crucified, dead Jew!" The courageous pastor jumped to his feet. In resounding tones he said, "Yes sir, I should indeed be a fool if I believed in a crucified, dead Jew. But, sir, *I believe in the living, risen Son of God.*" So do we. There is all the difference in the world between the two.

Devotion 44

"Seest Thou This Woman?"

Luke 7:44–47

Seest thou this woman?" One senses a note of sarcasm in the question. "Seest thou this woman?" The man had seen nothing else for the past half hour.

One wonders why the Pharisee invited Jesus to his home in the first place. He offered Jesus none of the normal courtesies incumbent on a host. His behavior was a deliberate insult to his invited Guest. A thousand angels would have rushed to wash those feet, to give Him a welcoming embrace, to anoint Him with fragrant oil. The Pharisee, instead, had offered the Lord a gratuitous insult. And the Lord recognized it for what it was, and bided His time, for He loved this mean-minded man as much as He loved Peter, James, and John. When He spoke, it would be as opportunity gave occasion and with a deep desire to save this small man's soul.

"Seest thou this woman?" She had set before the haughty, self-righteous Pharisee a threefold lesson; and the Lord picked it up at once and applied it to the Pharisee in a threefold repetition of the little word "but."

The woman presented *a lesson in contrition.* "Thou gavest me no water for my feet: *but* she hath washed my feet with her tears, and wiped them with the hairs of her head," Jesus said. "A broken and a contrite heart, O God," said the penitent psalmist, "thou wilt not despise" (Ps. 51:17). "She is a sinner!" That was all the Pharisee saw, a woman of the streets who had come into his house uninvited and whom he despised and would gladly have whipped and thrown back onto the street. The Pharisee curled his lips in a sneer. "This man is no prophet," he confided to himself, "or He would have known her for a sinner."

Well, God be praised, that is exactly what He did know. He accepted her tears of contrition as fitting tribute to Himself, the one who came into the world to save sinners.

The woman also provided *a lesson in consecration.* "Thou gavest me no kiss: *but* this woman since the time I came in hath not ceased to kiss my feet," Jesus said. She dared not give Him the customary kiss upon the cheek, so down she went at His feet, taking the place of a conquered captive. All her misdirected love was now channeled aright. She was His slave. She kissed His feet in total surrender, while the Pharisee shuddered in his shriveled soul, thinking not of consecration but of contamination. What would all his friends say, knowing he had a woman like that in his house?

Finally, this woman gave *a lesson in coronation.* "My head with oil thou didst not anoint: *but* this woman hath anointed my feet," Jesus declared. She recognized Him as the Christ, the Lord's Anointed. She poured her ointment over His feet. She crowned Him Lord of all, and Jesus sent her away in peace. Peace means the war is over. From now on, she had a new Lord, a new love, and a new life. As for Simon the Pharisee, it seems, the Lord had no more to say to him.

Devotion 45

THREE RICH MEN

LUKE 12:16–21; 16:19–31; 18:18–30

This is the story of three rich men. It could be that the references are all to the same person, at different stages in his career, and we will take them as such. Three phrases sum up the story of this individual—Too much! Too hard! Too late! We see him as a young man, as a middle-aged man, and as a dead man.

As a young man, he was rich, eager, and very likable (Luke 18:18–30). We are told that Jesus looked at him and loved him (Mark 10:21). Of course, Jesus loves all people; but here was a special case, like that of Martha, Mary, and Lazarus and like that of John, "the disciple whom Jesus loved." The young man had everything. He was *rich*. He was *respected* for, like Nicodemus, he was a ruler of the Jews. He was *religious* and even claimed to have kept all God's commandments. He was *restive*; he was aware that there was something lacking in his life, and he came to Jesus to find out what it was. He found out, soon enough. You love your neighbor as yourself, do you? Well, prove it. Sell all you have and share it with the poor. You love God with all your heart, do you? Then prove it. Come and follow Me to Calvary. The Lord was asking for *too much*. The young man turned away. The price was too high.

Later in his life, he has a problem (Luke 12:16–21). His fields had produced bumper crops. What was he to do with all his goods? Help the poor? Not him! That thought never occurred to him. He was too hard. He would build bigger and better barns. That was his proposal. He would store the grain until prices went up in the winter or until a drought year sent grain prices soaring. More! He would enjoy himself, he would have fun, and he would eat, drink, and be merry.

The plight of the poor did not interest him. He had proved that already when, as a rich young ruler, he had come to Christ and claimed to have kept the commandments, only to be exposed to the fact that he had no real feeling for the poor and disadvantaged. By now he was *too hard*. He had cultivated an attitude of total indifference to the poor, even to the poor fellow who haunted the gate of his mansion. Complacently he settled down for the night, satisfied with himself. He composed himself to sleep. Little did he know what a fool he was. A voice rang out in the darkness. He would be dead before sunrise. "This night thy soul shall be required of thee: then whose shall those things be?"

At the end of his life, we find him in a lost eternity (Luke 16:19–31). He had allowed a beggar to starve to death at his gate. Now he was dead himself. He was in hell, and he was still very much alive. He could see and hear and feel. He could reason and remember. Moreover, he was in torment. He tried to *pray*. He begged for some alleviation of his sufferings, but his request was denied. It was *too late*. Praying time was over. There was easy access to God on earth, but no access at all in hell. There was "a great gulf fixed."

He wanted to *preach*. "I have five brothers," he said. "Send Lazarus to them. They know Lazarus. They passed him often enough by my gate when they came to my house." His request was denied. "They have Moses and the prophets," he was told. "They have the Bible." "But they don't believe it, and they won't read it," the man cried, "but they would believe a man risen from the dead!" "If they will not believe the Bible, neither will they believe if one were to be raised from the dead," he was told. And that was that. It was too late.

Interestingly enough, the next man Jesus raised from the dead was a man named *Lazarus* (John 11). So stubborn was the unbelief of the Jewish leaders that they actually tried to put Lazarus back to death (John 12:10). The Lord was right. Though one arose from the dead they would not believe.

That remains true to this day. One of the best-documented and best-proved facts of history is the resurrection of Christ from the dead. Hundreds saw Him. His resurrection was public knowledge. The testimony of the four Gospels would be accepted as true in any court of law if put to the test using the same laws of evidence used in our courts today.

But will they believe? To this day thousands reject or ignore the fact that Jesus arose from the dead. How terribly sad that is.

Devotion 46

The Prayers of the Prodigal

Luke 15:12, 19

The Prodigal Son had two prayers. First, there was his *going away prayer*: "Father, give me." It was a wicked, selfish prayer, the prayer of a young man tired of restraint and tired of religion. He was tired, too, of his relations, his father who reined him in and his brother who ran him down. Indeed, one can feel sorry for any boy who has an older brother like the prodigal's—a smug, self-satisfied hypocrite and snob. It would be enough to make anyone with red blood in his veins run away. That Pharasaical elder brother of his made the world and its ways very attractive to the Prodigal Son.

So the prodigal responded to *the call of the world.* The far country beckoned, all smiles and good cheer. It offered freedom from all the restrictions of a godly home. It offered a wide gate and a broad highway where sin was called by other, friendlier names.

He responded, too, to *the congratulations of the world.* He headed for the far country with plenty of money in his pocket. He had youth and charm, and he paid generously for all his fair-weather friends to have their fun. So, for as long as his money lasted, it was wine, women, and song, a fast life, and plenty of laughs. But then his money ran out. At once the world turned a different face toward him.

He began to learn something of *the cares of this world.* A famine arose, and even capable, local men were thrown out of work. He felt the pinch of poverty. He was hungry. Nobody gave him so much as a dime. His fast-living friends abandoned him. He was out of work and out of money and far from home. He was lonely and hungry and cold.

He learned, too, in that far country, in Corinth, perhaps, or Athens, or Rome, or wherever it was he went, something of *the coldness of the world.* Gone were its smiles; gone was its song. He stood amid busy, bustling throngs and starved. "He joined himself," Jesus said, "to a citizen of that country" (Luke 15:15), but starvation wages were all he could earn. And what a job it was! He was hired to feed swine. What depths of disgrace this was for a well-born Jew! Feeding swine! Worse still, he became so hungry that he longed to eat the slops in the pig pail. So much for his going away prayer.

Now comes his *coming home prayer*: It was no longer, "Father, *give* me" but "Father, . . . *make* me as one of thy hired servants." His father's servants lived like lords of the land, well housed, well paid, well dressed, well fed—while he perished with hunger. "He came to himself," Jesus said (Luke 15:17). And then he came to the father. "I am no more worthy to be called thy son," he said. "Make me as one of thy hired servants."

We can picture the boy as he bangs on the door of the big house on the hill in that faraway land. "Here, Mister, here's your pig pail, and thanks for nothing. I'm going home to my father." The man would look him up and down with scorn, taking in his unwashed body, his unkempt beard, the marks of dissipation on his face. "Well, boy," he would say, "more the fool you are. If I were your father, I'd set the dogs on you." And the boy would say: "I daresay you would, but you don't know my father."

Nor did the prodigal for that matter. When he finally arrived home, it was not the servant's hall to which he was sent. He was caught in the father's embrace. The robe and the ring and the fatted calf were his, and new life as well. And the whole priceless story from the lips of the Lord is a parable of God's dealings with us.

Devotion 47

At the Cross

Luke 23:33–49

The world was at the cross. There were Jews present in Jerusalem from all parts of Palestine and from the remotest regions of the Diaspora. The titles, nailed to the cross of Jesus, were written in Greek and Latin and Hebrew, the three world languages of the day—Greek, the language of reason; Latin, the language of rule; Hebrew, the language of religion. Moreover, it was Passover time, and the normal population would be increased many times over by visitors from abroad. The world was at the cross—drawn to Canaan by the season and drawn to Calvary by the Savior, He who said: "And I, if I be lifted up from the earth, will draw all men unto me" (John 12:32). Luke tells us of some who were there.

First, *the Romans were there.* The Romans represented the vast, lost Gentile world. Their empire was full of pagans. They picture "the untold millions still untold," the multiplied millions of mankind without God, without Christ, and without hope. The Romans were there with their gift for government; with their military might; with all their pomp and power; with their engineering, technology, and science. They were able to conquer the world but unable to conquer themselves. They were practical and powerful but pagan. Calvary drew the likes of them.

Then, too, *the robbers were there.* The robbers represented the criminal class, those who defied the law, people who were guilty of open sins, brigands, insurrectionists, murderers, and the like. They had been caught red-handed in their crimes. They had been condemned. They were now paying the price of their sin. The robbers were there, hurling insults in the face of God by reviling His Son.

The rabble was there, too, the thoughtless, fickle mob. Jesus had healed their sick and raised their dead. He had fed their hungry multitudes, and cast out tormenting demons who possessed them. He had made their lame to walk, their blind to see, their dumb to speak, and their deaf to hear. They repaid Him by shouting for His death and by clamoring for the release of an insurrectionist and murderer, Barabbas by name. Now they were at Calvary to mock and jeer.

Most tragic of all, *the rabbis were there*—the rabbis with half the Bible memorized and the other half ignored. The rabbis had so tinkered with the Holy Scriptures that they had virtually buried the Bible beneath vast mountains of oral tradition. The rabbis were there to make quite sure that Jesus was dead so they could then go home to religiously keep the Sabbath and the Passover and imagine they had done God a favor. They were there mocking the Lord of Glory because He had saved others but could not save Himself.

So people came to Calvary, and the cross exposed them all. To the Jews that cross was a scandal to suggest that the Messiah of Israel could die on a Roman tree under the curse of God. To the Greeks the cross made no sense. To them it was the height of folly to preach "Christ and Him crucified." To the Romans, the cross of Christ was just another gibbet. They would scoff at a King of the Jews nailed to a cross. Ah, but unto us who are saved by the blood that was shed on that cross, the cross is both the power of God and the wisdom of God. It is God's answer to our sin. Our reaction to the preaching of the cross reveals our state of soul (I Cor. 1:18–25).

Devotion 48

CALVARY AND THE OFFERINGS

LUKE 24:25–27

At 6:00 AM the *burnt offering* was offered.[1] The burnt offering was all for God. It was an offering that depicted Jesus as one who was "obedient unto death, even the death of the cross" (Phil. 2:8). The sacrifice must be declared perfect, without spot or blemish. The exploring knife opened up the inward parts for inspection. The devouring flame caused the sweet-smelling savor of the sacrifice to ascend to God. It was at about this time of day that Jesus stood before Pilate, who pronounced Him sinless: "I find no fault in this man," he declared (Luke 23:4).

At 9:00 AM the *meal offering* was presented. The meal offering was of fine flour, ground until it was free from unevenness. It was then mixed with oil. It represents the perfect life of Christ energized by the Holy Spirit. There was no leaven in the meal offering (leaven is always a symbol of sin) and no honey (a symbol of mere natural sweetness) to be added to this offering. No energy of the flesh was even present in the life of the Lord Jesus. All was energized by the Spirit of God. The meal offering is described as "an offering made by fire, of a sweet savour unto the LORD" (Lev. 2:9). It points to Christ who, having been declared faultless by Pilate, was handed over to him to suffering and death.

At 12:00 PM the *peace offering* was offered. By that time, the Lord Jesus had been on the cross for three hours. At noon the darkness came down upon the scene as the Lord Jesus "made peace through the blood of his cross" (Col. 1:20). He was "made . . . sin for us" (2 Cor. 5:21) so that sin, which God hates, might be dealt with once and for all. Peace means that the war is over. The peace offering brought God and man together around the table. It became the foundation of a feast—but at uttermost

---

1. I am indebted to Ed Vallowe, a preacher friend of mine and one of the best informed students of the Word I know, for the information regarding the timing of the daily sacrifices.

cost to the ox or the lamb that was offered. Thus our Lord, who endured the cross, despising the shame, now ensures our peace with God and brings us into His banqueting house, where His banner over us is love.

At 3:30 PM the *sin offering* was offered. This was the offering that dealt with the *principle* of sin. "I am not a sinner because I sin; I sin because I am a sinner." We are like an apple tree, which is not an apple tree because it bears apples; it bears apples because it is an apple tree. We do what we do because we are what we are. The sin offering was designed to deal with our sin nature. At 3:00 PM Jesus said, "It is finished" (John 19:30). The work was done. Atonement had been made. Sin's awful price was paid in full.

At 6:00 PM the *trespass offering* was made. The trespass offering dealt with the *practice* of sin, with sin against another person. The sin offering dealt with our sin; the trespass offering deals with our sins. By 6:00 PM, the time when the trespass offering was sacrificed, the sufferings of Christ were all over. The Lord Jesus was already in the tomb of His fellow man.

The law of the trespass offering required that full restoration be made to the one who had been harmed. More, an additional fine was added so that the victim became the gainer. The Lord arose from that borrowed tomb of His, and both God in heaven and the believer on earth become gainers. God became a gainer because Calvary had provided Him with an adequate stage upon which He could demonstrate His love. God's wisdom and His power are adequately displayed in creation; His love is seen in our redemption.

Man has become a gainer too because of Calvary. Adam, we may suppose, could have remained in Eden for a million years and then have fallen into sin and died. The salvation Jesus procured for us places us forever beyond the reach of sin and death. If, on the other hand, neither Adam nor his posterity had ever sinned, his offspring would continue to be children of Adam, nothing more. By virtue of Calvary we become children of God and joint heirs with Jesus Christ. Moreover, we are seated in the heavenlies, exalted on high. All this lay latent in symbolic teaching of that final offering of the day.

Devotion 49

The Wedding at Cana

John 2:1–11

It is a memorable fact that the Lord's first public miracle was performed at a wedding and His last public miracle was performed at a funeral. Thus we see Him as Master of every situation—at life's gladdest hour and at life's saddest hour.

There are two things we might observe about the wedding at Cana. First, there are *the wedding guests.* It says something for the bride and groom that they invited Jesus and His disciples to their wedding. How thankful they must have been when the crisis arose that they had included Him when they thought of their marriage feast. And He came! Of course, He did, as He comes to every wedding to which He is called. And He came to bless.

John tells us nothing about the ceremony, nothing about the bride and groom, and nothing about the other guests, save for Mary. From the prominence of Mary and the way she spoke to the servants, this may have been the wedding of one of her nephews or nieces, or even, perhaps, that of one of her children. Tradition gives the names of Esther and Thamar to the sisters of Jesus. His brothers were James, Joses, Simon, and Judas (Matt. 13:55). Perhaps it was one of these who was getting married that day. Whoever the bride and groom were, they knew Jesus and He was their specially invited wedding guest.

Then there was *the wedding gift.* No doubt the couple received many wedding gifts that day; Jesus kept His until last. The wedding took place, and the banquet began. Then tragedy struck. Someone whispered to Mary—"We've run out of wine." In those days, and to this day in Eastern lands, lavish hospitality was a sacred duty. Gloom, mortification, and bitter, indelible disgrace was about to ruin everything. Total calamity loomed.

"They have no wine!" As F. W. Boreham says somewhere in one of his books, life always breaks down on the side of its exhilarations, its excitements, its joys. Mary passed on the sad news to Jesus. He gently disengaged Himself from anything that might have suggested He acted on her request or wish. He knew too well how far some would go in the coming ages to promote her instead of Him.

Then He went to work, as He always does, quietly, competently, gloriously. There was plenty of water, even if there was no wine! He would simply turn the one into the other.

It is a long, slow process to make wine. A vine must be planted. Water and nourishment must be drawn up from its roots to its branches. The vine must produce flowers. Insects must come and pollinate the plant. Little clusters of emerging grapes must appear. They must grow as rain and sunshine do their work. When ripe, the grapes must be picked and crushed. The flowing juice must be put into vats. It must ferment to turn into wine. Jesus simply telescoped the whole process into a miracle. As someone has said,

> The simple water, touched by grace divine
> Owned its Creator, and blushed into wine.

It was not hard for Him. After all—is He not the Vine (John 15:1)? No doubt the bride and groom never stopped thanking their special *wedding guest* for His special *wedding gift.*

Devotion 50

"How Can a Man Be Born When He Is Old?"

JOHN 3:4

It was a startled old man who asked the question: "How can a man be born when he is old?" The young prophet from Nazareth had shaken him to the core. We gather some information about the man right from the start. We know he was rich, respected, and religious. Edersheim tells of a Nicodemus who is mentioned in the Talmud as one of the richest and most distinguished citizens of Jerusalem. There is no actual proof, however, that he was this Nicodemus. Still, our Nicodemus was rich enough to lavishly supply costly spices, later on, for the Lord's burial. Moreover, he was a member of the Sanhedrin, the self-governing body, which under the Romans was allowed to make and administer certain civic and religious laws.

Nicodemus came to Jesus, which was a daring thing to do. The Lord had just cleansed the temple of its concessions, an act that was tantamount to an open declaration of war with the Jewish authorities. Nicodemus was even willing to go so far as to own Jesus to be "a teacher come from God" (John 3:2), but he could not have been prepared for Jesus' uncompromising and revolutionary reply to his opening remarks. "Except a man be born again," Jesus said, "he cannot see the kingdom of God" (v. 3). A dozen words and Jesus swept away the very foundations of this old man's hopes of heaven. "How can a man be born when he is old?" Nicodemus asked. Jesus' words, though they startled Nicodemus, nevertheless struck a responsive chord in the old man's soul, and awoke in him a recognition of a deep need of something better than the legalism in which he had been raised. So instead of arguing about it, he at once asked how a man could experience a new birth. The Lord had put an unerring finger on his deepest spiritual need. It was a need he felt, but one that hitherto he had not been able to express. "How?" Nicodemus asked.

How indeed? Later on, when John wrote his gospel, he reduced the Lord's answer to a formula (John 1:11–13). In it, he first tells us what being born again is *not*. It is *not of blood*. That is to say it is *not of human descent*. Spiritual life is not something we inherit from our parents, however godly they might be. All we inherit from them is a fallen Adamic nature. Moreover, it is *not of the will of the flesh*. That is, it is not of human desire. A desire to be a member of God's family does not make one a child of God. A desire to be born a member of the royal family does not make one a child of a king. Then, too, it is *not of the will of man*. That is to say, it is *not of human determination*. No amount of resolve can bring it to pass. A person might say, "Resolved: I consider myself a member of the British royal family." Such a resolve would be completely foolish. To be a member of the British royal family, one must be born into the royal family. Similarly, to be a child of God, one must be born into God's family. One must be born again.

Now look at what being born again *is*. First, there is something we have to *believe*. We must "believe on his name." And what is His name? Jesus, of course! And that name simply means "Savior"—one who saves His people from their sins (Matt. 1:21). That is what we need, someone who can save us from sin's penalty, from its power, and ultimately from its very presence.

Then comes the next step. It is not enough to "believe." We also must *receive*. It is one thing for me to believe that Jesus is the Savior; it is another thing for me to know Him as *my* Savior. That happens when I "receive Him," by asking Him to come into my life.

I *believe!* I *receive!* That is our part. Then God says, "*Become!*" That is His part. The believing and receiving is what we have to do. Then God does what He alone can do: impart to us spiritual life, His life, the life of God; and we are instantly born into His family. We become a child of God. His Holy Spirit comes into our human spirit, and we are born again, born of God.

Devotion 51

A Very Popular Text

John 3:16

The Holy Spirit sums up God's work in *creation* in ten statements: "And God said" (Gen. 1). He sums up God's Word in *legislation* in ten commandments (Exod. 20). And here, in John 3:16, He sums up God's way of *salvation* in ten words: God—loved—world—gave—son—whosoever—believeth—perish—hath—life. Just ten words tell us how to live forever. They can be grouped into five pairs.

The source of it all. We notice, first, *the Giver*: "God." The Greek word is *theos,* the word used in the Greek Bible for the God of the Old Testament—for *Elohim,* the God who creates; for *Jehovah,* the God who covenants; and for *Adonai,* the God who commands. Such is the Giver. The question of human sin and eternal salvation did not take God by surprise. God had thought it all out before ever He fashioned Adam's clay.

Next, we have *the Gift.* God did not give an angel to be our savior. The One who came from heaven to accomplish our salvation is coequal, coeternal, and coexistent with the Father and the Spirit. He is uncreated and self-existent. He is omnipotent, omniscient, and omnipresent. He is the second person of the Godhead. That is the One who came into the world to save sinners. No wonder Paul teaches us to say: "Thanks be unto God for his unspeakable gift" (2 Cor. 9:15). It is, perhaps, just an incident of translation; but there are twenty-five words in John 3:16, and the center word is "Son." God makes His Son the center of everything.

The secret of it all. Here we have first the *great reality*—"God *loved.*" When young Henry Morehouse preached for a week in D. L. Moody's church in Chicago years ago, he preached every night on this text. He finished with these words: "I have been trying to tell you how much God loves you. If I could borrow Jacob's ladder and climb to the city of God and ask Gabriel, the herald angel, to tell me how much God loves the world, he would say: 'God so loved the world that He gave His only begotten Son.'"

Next, we have the *great result*—"God so loved . . . that he *gave* his only begotten Son." Salvation is so simple to obtain that anyone, man or woman, boy or girl, rich or poor, wise or foolish, can make it his or her very own. God offers it to us as a free and unconditional gift. All we have to do to receive a gift, and make it our own, is to accept it. All the world's false religions say that salvation has to be earned. God says that salvation is free.

The simplicity of it all. First we have the *response* of faith: "whosoever believeth." Everyone has the capacity to believe, to exercise faith. We exercise faith every day—when we send a letter, when we deposit money in the bank, when we board a plane. Every day, ordinary faith, such as we exercise in a doctor, a druggist, or a driver, becomes *saving* faith when it becomes faith in our Lord Jesus Christ.

Next, we have the *reward* of faith: "hath." The moment we believe, that moment we have eternal life. God says so. There are no conditions, there is no probation, and there are no strings attached. It is instantaneous and eternal. We "hath" eternal life.

The scope of it all. The promise applies to *all people universally*: "For God so loved the *world*." The Jews of Jesus' day thought God loved only them, that they had some kind of monopoly on God. Not so! His love is for everyone. To paraphrase the old children's chorus,

> Red and yellow, black and white,
> All are precious in His sight.[1]

The promise also applies to *all people individually*: "*whosoever* believeth in him." The response of the little lad, when he was asked what the word "whosoever" meant, is delightful. He said, "It sort of means everyone else, and me." That, indeed, is the scope of it.

The seriousness of it all. There is the possibility of ending up in *hell*. Mark that word "perish." It is a strong word in the Greek. It means to be lost in utter spiritual destitution. The word is used of the bursting of a wine cask. It implies "utter, incredible loss." No wonder this issue of salvation is so serious.

But there is also the prospect of ending up in *heaven*: "everlasting life." That does not just mean length of days. One of Sir Henry Rider

---

1. C. Herbert Woolston, "Jesus Loves the Little Children."

Haggard's most popular novels tells of a woman who lengthened her days for two thousand years—and she spent them in misery.[2] God offers us, not just a mere quantity of days, but life! Life marked by "joy unspeakable and full of glory!" His kind of life! What a prospect!

---

2. Sir Henry Rider Haggard, *She,* 1887.

Devotion 52

Light Is Come into the World

John 3:19

This is the condemnation," says John, "that light is come into the world, and men loved darkness rather than light, because their deeds were evil." This verse lives on the same street in Scripture as its famous neighbor, John 3:16, and only three verses down. It is a great text in its own right, despite the fact that we tend to overlook it. It takes us to the cradle, to the cross, and to the courtroom.

First, comes *the cradle*: "light is come into the world." That is John's description of the birth of Christ. Light! Light was the first thing God called into existence when He created the world. Everything about light is mysterious. It can pass unsullied through a dirty windowpane. Its speed is always constant, some 186,000 miles per second. It is the great invariable in a world of constant motion, shifting patterns, and endless change.

Jesus, the Light of the World, is always the same. He is, "the same, yesterday, and to day, and for ever" (Heb. 13:8). When on earth He treated all people with the same unwavering honesty, love, holiness, and courtesy. He loved the elder brother just as much as He loved the runaway prodigal. He loved that scheming scoundrel Caiaphas just as much as He loved the attentive Nicodemus.

At Bethlehem God wrapped up deity in humanity. He appeared as a little babe, dressed in swaddling clothes, lying in a manger! Or, to follow John's approach, at Bethlehem God lit a little candle, and light came into the world. Satan thought it would be a good thing to extinguish that light before it flooded all the world. He made sure he had his man in place, a monster by the name of Herod. But Herod's murderers arrived too late. The light had been removed to Egypt. Now that light is everywhere. It shows us where we are and what we are, how lost we are and how dark a place this world is.

Next comes *the cross*: "men loved darkness rather than light, because their deeds were evil." The Lord's goodness exposed their badness. His honesty exposed their hypocrisy. His holiness exposed their wickedness. The authority of His teaching exposed their emptiness. Their answer was to get rid of Him. "This is your hour, and the power of darkness," He told them (Luke 22:53). They lied about Him, hired false witnesses against Him, and crucified Him.

But, even on the cross, Jesus demonstrated who He really was and who, in fact, was in control. He put out the sun, and total darkness reigned for three long hours. Then, as a parting gift, just before He died, He turned the light back on again. Then He died, and the *true* Light went out, not for a brief three hours, but for three whole days. Then, back He came! The darkness could not conquer the light after all.

This brings us to *the courtroom*. Now Jesus sits upon His Father's throne in heaven, in a light beyond the brightness of the noonday sun. One day the Christ-rejecting millions will be summoned to stand in the full blaze of that light, to be exposed, and then to be expelled to the blackness of darkness forever.

One last thought. We can shut the daylight out, but we cannot shut it in. Those who have come to the light and embraced the light will *shine*. They will "walk in the light, as he is in the light" (I John 1:7), and they will find that "the path of the just is as the shining light, that shineth more and more unto the perfect day" (Prov. 4:18).

Devotion 53

My Father's House

John 14:1–6

I'm going back home!" Jesus said. The disciples were stunned. Ever since His unveiling on the Mount of Transfiguration, He had been preparing them for the news; but, even so, it was like a bombshell. He sat down and sought to comfort them. We look first at their *broken hearts.* "Let not your heart be troubled," He said. The word for "troubled" here is the same word used of the reaction of the disciples sometime before, when they saw Him walking toward them over a wild and stormy sea. They thought He was a ghost. They were "troubled," agitated. But it was Jesus! He stilled the storm and landed them safely on the distant shore. As then, so now! All was well. He'd see them safely home. In the meantime His promise is sure. "I will not leave you comfortless [lit., as orphans]," He said.

Now let us look at their *better home.* When the queen of Sheba saw the glory of Solomon, including the golden temple and the king's own magnificent palace, she was overwhelmed. "The half was not told me," she said (I Kings 10:7). We too will be awed by the indescribable glory of our home on high. He, the great Carpenter of Nazareth, has been working on that place now for some two thousand years.

"I go to prepare a *place* for you," He said. The word for "place" is of interest. It is *topos,* which gives us our word "topography." It suggests a geographical, topographical location. It reinforces the fact that He is preparing a real place for real people.

"I go to prepare a place for *you,*" He said. This place is not a home for the heavenly hosts on high. They already have their own estate. This place is for us. How Satan must gnash his teeth in rage as he catches glimpses of the ivory palaces, the Edenic parks, and the countless wonders of that glorious place the Son of God is preparing for us! Adding bitterness to that pill he is forced to swallow is the fact that he is powerless to wreck and ruin that world the way he has wrecked and ruined this one.

But we can take yet another look: "I will come again, and receive you unto myself; that where I am, there ye may be also." This points us to our *blessed hope.* Just as Jesus came to earth the first time to literally fulfill all the promises concerning His coming to redeem, so He will come back again to literally fulfill all the promises concerning His coming to reign. There is more in the Bible about His coming again than about any other theme. It is mentioned 1,845 times in the Old Testament and 318 times in the New. It is found in 27 of the 39 Old Testament books and in 17 of the 27 New Testament books.

"I'm coming!" He says. As the old hymn puts it:

Midst the darkness, storm and sorrow
One bright gleam I see,
Well I know the blessed morrow
Christ will come for me. . . .

He, who in His hour of sorrow
Bore the curse alone,
I who in the lonely desert
Trod where He had gone.

He and I in that bright glory
One deep joy shall share
Mine to be for ever with Him
His that I am there.[1]

1. Gerhardt Tersteegen, "Midst the Darkness, Storm and Sorrow."

Devotion 54

WITNESSES UNTO ME

ACTS 1:8

For a period of forty days, between firstfruits and Pentecost, the risen Lord tarried here on earth. Over yonder the standards of the Almighty were unfurled. To the utmost bounds of the everlasting hills, the heralds had borne the news: "The Lord is risen indeed." The morning stars sang together, and all the sons of God shouted for joy. Twelve legions of angels were drawn up in battle array along the jasper battlements of heaven and at the gates of pearl. Eager eyes were watching. But still he did not come. Still He tarried, even though His own heart was hungry for home. He stayed because He had one more thing to do—prepare the disciples for the task He had in mind.

First, they needed *enlistment,* so He made His *passion* known to them. He wanted them to reach "the uttermost part of the earth." They were to witness to Him in Jerusalem, in Judea, in Samaria, and to Earth's remotest bounds. They were to meet a man from Ethiopia and a man from Macedonia. They were to meet men and women, boys and girls from all parts of the world. It was to be the whole duty of the whole church for the whole age. That was His passion. The whole world must know the good news that Christ died for their sins, that He was buried, and that He rose again.

Moreover, they needed *encouragement,* so He made His *presence* known to them. He Himself would be with them, always, and to the end of the world. So He showed Himself alive, after His passion, "by many infallible proofs" (Acts 1:3). The task was thus simplified. They were not called to preach a dogma or a creed or found a new religion. They were called to preach Christ, to tell people of a living, relevant Person. They were to make Him real to other people. However, before they could make Him real to anyone else, He had to be real to them. So the Lord appeared here and showed up there. He made Himself real to this one and to that one. They needed to become convinced of His abiding presence, that He was there, alongside them, whether seen or unseen. He was there as He promised He would be to the end of time (Matt. 28:19–20). He appeared to each in a different way. With Mary, it was the whisper of her name. With the Emmaus disciples, it was the exposition of the Word. With Thomas, it was His hands and feet and side. By the time He was through, they were all convinced of the reality of His resurrection, His rapture, and His return.

Then, too, they needed *enlightenment*, so He made His *program* known to them. They were to begin in their own community, Jerusalem. They were to reach their own province, Judea. They were to evangelize their own continent, beginning with Samaria, the closest alien culture. They were to reach the whole, wide world. That was the plan. The book of Acts shows how closely and how successfully that plan was followed.

Finally, they needed *enablement*, so He made His *power* known to them. He set before them the impossible task of persuading people to repent of their sins, to turn to Christ, and to accept Him by faith and have their lives transformed. The problem was that they were powerless to witness. When Mary Magdalene, Joanna, Mary the mother of Jesus, and other women told the Twelve that Jesus was alive, "their words seemed to them as idle tales, and they believed them not" (Luke 24:11). When the Emmaus disciples arrived back in Jerusalem with the news of a risen Christ, "neither believed they them" (Mark 16:13). When all ten of the other disciples tried to convince Thomas, he said, "I will not believe." They needed enablement.

"Ye shall receive power," Jesus said, "after that the Holy Ghost is come upon you." And so they did! For it is only the Holy Spirit who can make Christ real to an unregenerate and disbelieving heart. And that is exactly what He did on the day of Pentecost, and with such phenomenal success that thousands were swept into the kingdom of heaven that same day.

Devotion 55

I Must See Rome

Romans 1:10–13

Paul had never been to Rome. The church in that great city probably had been founded by Jews converted under Peter's preaching on the day of Pentecost. Peter should have written to the Romans. But he didn't. Peter was a big man in Jerusalem, but it took a much bigger man to write to Rome.

Although Paul had never been to Rome, he had an intense interest in the place. Indeed, some of his converts were there. Doubtless his fame had already reached the church at Rome because news and information traveled fast on the great highways of the empire. Scraps of truth from his preaching and his pen had likely already reached Rome. Echoes of the controversy against him, stirred up by the legalists, had doubtless also reached the capital. He himself wanted to come there, and he decided to write to the Roman church. Naturally he began by introducing himself. He says three things about himself and his longing for Rome.

He begins with *his divine authority*. He was a *servant,* he says, a slave, a bond slave of Jesus Christ (Rom. 1:1). No man valued his freedom more than Paul. "I was free born," he declared to Claudius Lysias (Acts 22:28). Just the same he was the willing slave of Christ. When in prison he never regarded his chains as the bonds of Caesar. They were "his bonds in Christ," the badge of his total commitment to the Lord.

He was an *apostle,* the equal of Peter, James, and John (Rom. 1:1). He was God's sent one, with all the power and authority of an apostle and with the Gentile world as his field.

And he was "*separated.*" He was separated by God *before his birth* (Rom. 1:1). He was separated by Christ *at his conversion.* He was separated by the Holy Spirit *at his commissioning* for world evangelism (Acts 9:15; 13:2; Gal. 1:15). He was armed with authority from God.

Second, there was *his definite ambition.* He wanted to go to Rome. He had put "Rome" at the top of his proposed itinerary every time he set out on another crusade. But God had always held him back. Now Paul signs a blank check. He asks God to write in the amount, no matter what the cost, for him to go to Rome. "By any means!" he says (Rom. 1:10). Not long afterward, God filled in the amount and sent Paul to Rome—in chains. Paul never complained about that. At least he was in Rome and able to reach out from there.

Third, there was *his doctrinal argument*. Paul mentions the *supremacy* of the gospel: "I am not ashamed of the gospel," he says (Rom. 1:16). The gospel dealt with facts superior to anything known to Greek logic, with a force superior to all Rome's legions, and with a faith superior to anything known to Jewish light.

Paul proclaimed that gospel everywhere—in Jerusalem, the religious capital of the world; in Athens, the intellectual capital of the world; and in Rome, the imperial capital of the world. At Jerusalem he was mobbed, at Athens he was mocked, and at Rome he was martyred. But still the gospel reigned supreme.

He mentions, moreover, the *sufficiency* of the gospel. It stirs the mind, it satisfies the heart, it subdues the will, it searches the conscience, it saves the soul, and it sanctifies the life. "It is the power of God unto salvation," Paul said.

And he mentions the simplicity of the gospel. It is "to every one that believeth." All it calls for is simple, childlike trust in God, whose word is sacred and can never be broken. Simple? Yes, indeed!

A little child of seven,
Or even three or four,
Can enter into heaven,
Through Christ the open door.

Simple? Yes! But also sublime. Mark the weighty words Paul uses in his introduction alone: gospel, Christ, power, God, salvation, everyone, believeth, Jew, Gentile, righteousness, revealed, faith, just, and live. There is enough truth in those fourteen words to occupy our minds for a lifetime!

"I must see Rome!" Paul said. God kept him waiting, because, except for Jerusalem, Rome was the most dangerous place in the world for Paul. Besides, it would be good for the gospel, for the churches, and for Christians in Rome to have an inspired epistle to prepare them for this intrepid apostle.

Devotion 56

The Four Faces of Self

Romans 6–7

By the time Paul arrived at Romans 6, he had the answer to the sovereignty of self in the soul of a saint. He tells us that we are not free *to* sin but are free *from* sin. We who once were dead *in* sin are now dead *to* sin. The Lord of Glory, who gave His life *for* us, now lives, in the power of resurrection, to give His life *to* us. It is a matter of the right use of the humble preposition.

That is very good news indeed. It is such good news that Paul presents it to us in four unforgettable illustrations. He tells us, first, that the old nature in the believer is like *an old man,* a wicked old man. Scofield renders Paul's expression, "the old man," more vividly as "the man of old," the man we used to be. We are born with a fallen nature, a nature that can do nothing right. We are born again with a divine nature, a nature that can do nothing wrong. The two natures are at war. But here is God's answer to "the old man" and his deeds: *the old man is now dead.* He is "crucified with Christ."

We find it hard to believe such an awesome truth because the old nature doesn't *feel* dead. Feelings, however, do not alter facts. God says that the old nature is dead, and the whole machinery of redemption operates on the assumption that God says what He means and means what He says. We must take God at His word in all this.

Next, Paul says the old nature in the believer is like *an old monarch.* God gave dominion over everything to Adam, but when tempted, Adam surrendered his sovereignty to Satan. As a result, we were born into a world controlled by the Evil One. We were born subject to sin, self, and Satan. *The old monarch, however, is now defeated.* At Calvary the Lord Jesus triumphed gloriously over Satan and despoiled principalities and powers. Every believer is automatically constituted a citizen of the kingdom of God. "Let not sin therefore reign," Paul says (Rom. 6:12). "Sin shall not have dominion over you," he adds (v. 14). We must take God at His word.

Then, too, the old nature is like *an old master.* We were born slaves to sin, a bondage into which we were sold by Adam. We have inherited his fallen, sinful nature. We know by bitter experience the bondage of evil habits. Two thousand years ago, however, the Lord Jesus came into the slave market of sin and paid the price of our redemption. He purchased us at infinite cost, with His own blood, and has set us free. *So, the old master is now deposed.* We no longer need to obey its wicked demands. "Being then made free from sin," says Paul, "ye became the servants of righteousness," servants of God no less (v. 18).

Finally, the old nature is likened to *an old marriage.* When Adam fell, the whole human race was potentially in him. As a result, all his posterity are born married, as it were, to sin, and what a hideous and hateful marriage it is! We live on the most intimate terms with sin. We go to bed with it at night. We get up with it in the morning. We live with it moment by moment throughout the day. Consciously or carelessly we live as those who are married to sin. *But this old marriage is now dissolved.* Not only did our death with Christ put an end to the old marriage, but we are now "married to another, even to him who is raised from the dead" (7:4). Now we live in intimacy with that glorious Man who reigns on high and, in consequence of this intimacy, bring forth fruit unto God. An old man, now dead! An old monarch, now defeated! An old master, now deposed! An old marriage, now dissolved! What more could we want than that?

Devotion 57

SONS OF GOD

ROMANS 8:14–39

When the widow Douglas adopted Huckleberry Finn, it turned out to be a painful process for the boy. His father had been the town drunk and the boy himself was a picturesque prodigal. His home was an old hogshead and his food such scraps as he could scrounge. His spicy language was the delight of all the other boys and the horror of their parents. His pipe, his tattered ruin of rags that constituted his wardrobe, and his unkempt person did not qualify him for society.

The widow set about adopting him and then adapting him. He had to be washed and dressed in clothes that tortured him and shod with shoes that cramped him. He had to sleep in a bed at night, sit up at a table for his meals, and use a knife and fork. The whole process hurt.

When God adopts us into His family, it is the same. We have to be adapted to our new life in Christ. So the Holy Spirit sets to work on us. We have to be groomed for glory.

Let us meditate on what it means to be placed into God's family as adult children by the process of adoption. Three things happen. First, *we are led by the Spirit* (v. 14). We who have been adopted into God's family have this common trait: we are guided through life by the Spirit of God. Even though we may stumble and fall, nevertheless, obedience to the Spirit is the main trend of our life. Take the Mississippi River, for instance. Even though it flows southward, there are places where it flow eastward and even northward. But these are only temporary aberrations. The main southward direction of the flow always takes over in the end. It is just so with a child of God. The true flow of a believer's life is toward holiness, even though there may be occasional lapses. In time the flow heavenward and homeward is resumed.

Then, too, *we are loved by the Father* (vv. 15–16). The Holy Spirit bears witness to that along with our human spirit. Paul says we are to address

God as "Abba Father." *Abba* is an Aramaic word that expresses the cry of an infant. It is the word of unquestioning trust. The word *Father* comes from the Greek (*pater*). It is the form of address used by an adult son who is able to enter into the heart, mind, and will of the father. Jesus used both words in Gethsemane. It is proof of our sonship that we can do the same.

Finally, *we are lifted by the Son* (v. 17). "If children, then [we are] heirs; heirs of God, and joint-heirs with Christ." Paul adds, "if so be that we suffer with him, that we may be also glorified together." There is always a strong link in the Bible between the sufferings of Christ and the glory that is to follow. We see this principle illustrated in the lives of Peter and Paul. Peter was a witness of the sufferings and a partaker of the glory (on the Mount of Transfiguration). Paul was a witness of the glory (on the Damascus road) and a partaker of the sufferings. God allows us to suffer in order to purify us and lift us.

When God met Jacob at the Jabbok, He broke him in order to bless him (Gen. 32:24–32). Carnal, scheming, self-willed Jacob was renamed "Israel." He was proclaimed to be a prince, having "power with God and with men." This crisis experience, however, was followed by a long, slow process of adapting Jacob. It took time. It always does. There are no shortcuts to a holy life.

In chapter after chapter of Genesis, we see the process. There was the defilement of Jacob's daughter (something that must have broken Jacob's heart). There was the duplicity of Simeon and Levi. There was the disgrace of Reuben, the degradation of Judah, the disappearance of Joseph, the detention of Simeon in Egypt, and the demand for Benjamin. The process went on and on. Nor do we see much change in Jacob, not until we get near the end.

In the closing chapters of Genesis, however, we see a different Jacob. We see a man adapted for glory. He too was in Egypt now. He was surrounded by wealth and opportunity. He was there for seventeen years and could have made his fortune. But his heart was in another land. His heart was in Canaan, untouched by all the gold and glamour of Egypt. More than that, we see him blessing Pharaoh on his throne and bearing witness to his pilgrimage. He was ready for heaven and home. So we learn that God adapts those He adopts and that He is never in a hurry. He takes His time.

Devotion 58

Eternal Security

Romans 8:28–39

In the closing section of his great treatise on the Christian life (Rom. 8), Paul deals with the security of the believer. We are *predestined for glory* (vv. 28–30), and we are *preserved for glory* (vv. 31–39). God knows all about us. Nothing happens by chance. Paul says, "We know that all things work together for good to them that love God, to them who are the called according to his purpose."

Here we have *a blessed assurance.* Paul says, "We know." We do not have to indulge in wishful thinking. God has spoken, and His Word cannot be broken. We have, moreover, *a basic assumption.* God says, "All things work together for good to them that love God, to them who are the called according to his purpose." All things work together for everyone, for better or for worse. All things work together for *good* for those who are *His people* and those who are in *His purpose.* Jacob, the Old Testament patriarch, shows us how all this works out in the end.

We see Jacob sitting in his tent, wringing his hands with grief. A great cry of despair breaks from his lips. Ever since he returned to the Promised Land, everything seems to have gone wrong. If any man was a man "called according to God's purpose," Jacob was that man. He was back in the land, back to the place where God had put His name and where He met with His people. But everything seems to have conspired against him.

He had narrowly escaped being plundered by Laban, his unscrupulous father-in-law. He had purchased his peace with Esau at great price, even though he could not be sure that Esau might not yet be back for more, backed by his four hundred fighting men. His only daughter had been seduced and disgraced; and his sons Simeon and Levi had wreaked fearful vengeance on the man responsible. They had put the whole family in peril. His beloved Rachel had died, and his dear Joseph had disappeared and was presumed to be dead, torn to pieces by wild beasts. Judah, the best of a bad lot, had disgraced himself.

Now a famine is raging in the Promised Land, and keeping the family together requires that his sons go back to Egypt to buy more corn. Already his son, Simeon, has been detained in Egypt by the imperious grand vizier. Worse still, that despotic man has demanded that Benjamin be brought to Egypt as a hostage. Food is needed. The boys must go back for more, but they adamantly refuse to go back for more grain without Benjamin.

"All these things are against me," Jacob wailed. Little did he know that all things were working together for good! Joseph is alive and is seated at the right hand of power in Egypt, the very grand vizier Jacob dreads. Simeon is living off the fat of the land in Egypt. Soon the wagons will be coming to bring Jacob to Joseph's side. As the hymn writer would phrase it:

> Ye fearful saints, fresh courage take;
> The clouds ye so much dread
> Are big with mercy and shall break
> In blessings on your head.[1]

Yes, indeed! All things do work together for good for those who love God and who are wrapped up in His eternal purpose to bless His own! Dark as things may seem, there is another side to our circumstances—God's side.

> Not till the looms are silent
> And the shuttles cease to fly,
> Will God unroll the canvas
> And explain the reason why;
> The dark threads are as needed
> In the Weaver's skillful hand
> As the threads of gold and silver
> In the pattern He has planned.[2]

---

1. William Cowper, "God Moves in a Mysterious Way," 1774.
2. "The Plan of the Master Weaver" (author unknown).

Devotion 59

Who?

Romans 8:33–39

God throws down the gauntlet to all the enemies of His people. "Who," He says, "shall lay any thing to the charge of God's elect?" Satan comes, eager to take up the challenge. He comes as the *Accuser.* He is the ancient father of lies, well versed in the art of deceit. The great idiom of his language is the lie. "Tell a lie big enough, and often enough, and people will believe it," is his philosophy. However, when he comes into the presence of God, he does not come to tell lies. No lie can last a moment in the burning light in which God dwells. Moreover, sad to say, when he comes into the presence of God, Satan has no need to tell lies about us. He needs only to tell the truth about us. So he takes up the challenge. "Who shall lay any thing to the charge of God's elect?" "I will," Satan says, "as the Accuser of the brethren."

God throws down the gauntlet again. "Who," He says, "shall separate us from the love of Christ?" It is love as vast, as deep, and as wide as eternity. Satan comes again, this time as the *Adversary.* He has a thousand means at his command to torment, torture, and terrify that "feeble folk," as he sees them, who make up the ranks of the people of God.

But Satan does not have a chance. For be he Accuser or Adversary (Devil or Satan), he is confronted at once by the *Advocate* (I John 2:1).

"So," says our Advocate with the Father, "you are the Accuser, are you? Well, lay your charge." But even as Satan begins the sad tale of all the sins and shortcomings of even the saintliest of the people of God, he is put to silence. "You are talking of those whom God Himself has justified," the Advocate declares. He shows His hands still bearing the marks of Calvary, where the sin question was settled once and for all. "There are no such sins as those you mention. In fact, there are no sins at all. God remembers them no more"(Heb. 8:12; 10:17).

Satan tries again. "So," says our Advocate, "you have come back, have you? You are here now as the Adversary. You want to separate God's people from God's love. Impossible! What weapons do you have?"

"What about *the inevitable*? What about 'death or life'?"

"Death is no use to you because I have the keys of death. Life offers you no advantage, for I am the Life."

"What about *the invisible*? What about 'angels, principalities, and powers'?"

"At Calvary I made an open show of the likes of those" (Col. 2:15), says our Advocate.

"What about *the inescapable*? What about 'things present or things to come'?"

"I am the great I AM, the ever-present one; and I am the coming one. Nothing you have, now or then, will be of use to you."

"What about *the incalculable*? What about 'height or depth'?"

"I have been down to the deepest depths. I reign in the highest heights. You have no hope or advantage there," the Advocate declares.

"What about *the inconceivable*? What about 'any other creature'?"

"I am the Creator. There is no created being in the whole wide universe over which I do not exercise absolute power. As for you, you have no power. Nothing can separate mine from Me. Satan, you are a defeated foe," our Advocate says. And so he is!

Hallelujah! What a Savior!

Devotion 60

Our Lord Jesus Christ

Romans 16:18

Our Lord Jesus Christ: two opposite considerations draw out our thoughts at the mention of this name. In the first place, He is "our" Lord Jesus Christ. Evidently, the apostle is referring to the Christ of the *Christian,* but the context is quite different. The context has to do with those who embrace error, those who cannot correctly answer the Lord's own, piercing question: "What think ye of Christ? whose son is he?" (Matt. 22:42). For, in stark contrast with *our* Lord Jesus Christ, the Christ of the Christian, stands *their* Lord Jesus Christ, the christ of the cults.

Our Lord Jesus Christ is *Lord*—He is *the Master,* the One who controls all things. He is the creator and sustainer of all things. He is the sovereign Lord of the universe, the One at whose name every knee will One day bow, the One to whom every tongue will confess that He is Lord.

Our Lord Jesus Christ is beloved by all His own as *Jesus*—He is *the Man.* He became a man when He was born at Bethlehem, truly human in every sense of the word. He was born, He lived, He died, and He rose again. Now He is enthroned on high, and still He wears the scars of His sojourn on earth. Those scars are indelibly printed into His hands and feet and side. He knows what it is like to share our experiences as humans. He is sinless yet sympathetic, humble and holy, loving and lowly, patient and pure and kind. He is "Jesus!"

Our Lord Jesus is also the *Christ*—He is *the Messiah,* the Anointed One, prophet, priest, and king—a prophet to reveal, a priest to redeem, and a king to rule. Such is "our Lord Jesus Christ." "Our Lord Jesus Christ!" Such is His full and proper name.

Now let us consider the christ of the cults. There are the liberals, for instance, who have a christ, but He is not our Lord Jesus Christ. Their christ was conceived out of wedlock, supposedly by some passing liaison between Mary and an unknown soldier—and therefore is subject to the terrible excommunication inflicted on the illegitimate child by the Mosaic Law. Their christ performed no miracles, died as a martyr, and rose again only in legend. Their christ is not our Lord Jesus Christ. Pity them!

The Jehovah's Witnesses have a christ, but he is not God. Their christ did not rise from the dead. The body of their christ dissolved in gases in the tomb. Nor is their christ the second person of the Godhead, a member of the Trinity, the Creator of the universe. Their christ is not our Lord Jesus Christ. Pity them!

The Mormons have a christ. But their christ was a polygamist, secretly married to Martha and Mary. By no means is their christ "our Lord Jesus Christ."

"They that are such," says the Holy Spirit, "serve not our Lord Jesus Christ." Our Lord Jesus Christ is God the Son. He entered into human life by being virgin born. He lived a sinless life, performed countless miracles, and fulfilled scores of Old Testament prophecies. Our Lord Jesus Christ died an atoning death. He was buried and rose again the third day. He has ascended into heaven where He now sits at God's right hand as our Great High Priest, anticipating the day of His coming again. That is our Lord Jesus Christ.

Devotion 61

The Lord's Supper

1 Corinthians 11:23–34

Public worship reaches its climax at the Lord's Table, as we partake of the emblems on the table. We do so in remembrance of the Lord Jesus and because He requests it.

Exhorting one another in the things of God is not worship. Singing and special music do not in themselves constitute worship. Reciting specially chosen Scripture passages is not in itself worship. Following a carefully planned order of service does not guarantee worship. Listening to pulpit oratory is not worship. Praying for one another does not constitute worship. Being occupied with evangelism, soulwinning, missionary activity, and the like does not constitute worship. Of course, all these things may at times be elements of worship.

True worship is brought into true focus at the Lord's Table. There we are occupied with Jesus only. *That* is worship.

At the Lord's Table, we remember the Lord, in Spirit and in truth (John 4:24). That, of course, excludes all those who do not know Him. You cannot remember someone you do not know and have never met. Occupation with the Lord Jesus reaches its climax in partaking of the bread and of the wine. This is pure worship. It should be spontaneous, not arranged. It should be guided in all its parts (a carefully chosen and appropriate hymn here; a relevant Scripture reading there, with or without comment; now a prayer of praise and adoration, in keeping with the occasion) by the Holy Spirit.

Three elements are prominent in such worship. Paul reminds us that we are to be taken up with the Lord's *person*. Jesus, in instituting this feast of remembrance, said, "This do in remembrance of me." That opens up a vast field of worship. We can be taken up with the Lord's deity, with His humanity, His attributes, and His wisdom, with His love and power. We can be occupied with His eternal preexistence as God the

Son, second person of the Godhead. We can worship Him as Creator of the universe, the One who is adored and served by all the angel throng.

We can remember He is truly man. We can meditate on His incarnation; His life; His words and works; His death, burial, and resurrection; His oneness with the Father, with the Spirit, and with His bride. All these and many other things may be involved in remembering His person.

Moreover, we are to be taken up with the Lord's *passion*: "As often as ye eat this bread, and drink this cup, ye do show the Lord's death." This, too, opens up a vast field of worship. Many Old Testament types remind us of His death. The various offerings, for instance, the feasts, and truths connected with the tabernacle and its furniture. Such monumental passages as Psalm 22, Psalm 69, and Isaiah 53 all come to mind. So do the frequent references to the Lord's death in the Gospels and Epistles. We focus in worship on the events that surrounded the Lord's death, burial, and resurrection. We think of His sufferings, the events of His last crowded week on earth. We stand with Moses and Elijah on the holy mount as they talk with Him about His departure. We stand in Pilate's judgment hall. We journey from Gethsemane to Gabbatha to Golgotha and the grave. We remember His passion. Besides our open Bibles, a hundred hymns help us to remember.

But there is one thing more. We are to be taken up with the Lord's *position*. We remember Him thus "till He come." The Lord is no longer on the cross or in the tomb. He is seated at the right hand of the Majesty on high. He is our Advocate with the Father. He is our Great High Priest. He is coming again. All these things provide us with themes for worship.

Worship, after all, is the ascription of "worthship" to Him.

Devotion 62

He Was Seen

1 Corinthians 15:5–9

It has been said that the resurrection of Christ is the best-proven fact in history, that there is more documentary evidence for the resurrection of Christ than for the conquest of Britain by Julius Caesar.

Something *must* have happened. There on Calvary's hill a Man died on a Roman cross amid the mocking of rulers and rabbis alike. He was alone, rejected by men and abandoned by God. But look now! That very same Man who was murdered, mocked, and maligned is now worshiped by millions. Inside of fifty years, there was a church devoted to His worship in every major city of the Roman empire. Something *must* have happened in between. Something did! He arose from the dead. The Man who hung upon that Roman cross rose in splendor from the tomb. "I . . . have the keys," he says, "of hell and of death" (Rev. 1:18).

"He was seen," says Paul. Then he brings to our attention a body of competent and reliable eyewitnesses to that awesome event, witnesses whose testimony would stand up in any court of law in the civilized world.[1]

First, he was seen by His *friends,* by Peter and the other disciples. Consider Peter, for instance. Something must have happened to make that coward brave. One day we see him cringing before a housemaid and denying with oaths and curses that He even knew the Lord. A month and a half later he is seen preaching Christ boldly in Jerusalem, charging the Jews with the murder of their Messiah. What happened? He met the risen Christ!

---

1. Simon Greenleaf was the dean of the Harvard Law School in his day. He wrote a book on the laws of evidence that became a standard text for a century. He wrote another book in which he summoned the four evangelists into court and examined their testimony to Christ. His verdict was that their testimony was true. See Simon Greenleaf, *The Testimony of the Evangelists: Examined by the Rules of Evidence Administered in Courts of Justice* (1874; reprint, Grand Rapids: Baker, 1965).

He was seen "of the twelve," Paul adds, referring to the Lord's disciples. They all saw Him together on more than one occasion. On one such occasion, doubting Thomas changed his mind forever and owned the risen Christ as Lord and God.

Then, too, He was seen by the *faithful*. Paul mentions that He was seen by more than five hundred people at one time—most of whom Paul knew to still be alive when he wrote.

Moreover, He was seen by His *family*—in particular, by His skeptical and tough-minded brother, James. James had not believed the Lord's claims during His life, but he believed in them after he saw Him alive from the dead. James became a well-known figure in Jerusalem, on cordial terms with leading Jews and the acknowledged leader of the Jewish Christian community. The book he wrote testifies to James's total commitment to Christ. He was given undeniable personal proof that Jesus was alive. That is what transformed him.

The risen Christ was seen by His *followers*. "He was seen . . . of all the apostles," says Paul. Indeed, one essential requirement to be an apostle was that the person had to have seen the risen Christ.

Finally, He was seen by His *foe*. "Last of all he was seen of me," said Paul. Paul once had been the bitterest enemy of both Christ and the church. He was converted on the Damascus road while actively involved in an enterprise to persecute believers in Christ. There he came face to face with the risen Lord and was instantly transformed. He became the greatest of all the apostles of the Christian church.

Devotion 63

Love That Knows No Measure

Ephesians 3:17–19

Paul's prayer for us is that we might know the breadth, length, depth, and height of God's love. Many a person in Paul's place might have questioned God's love. After all, Paul was in prison in Rome, accused of high treason and awaiting trial before Nero. He was longing to be set free—either by *acquittal,* which would free him to get back into the thick of things, on the cutting edge of danger, blazing new gospel trails in "the regions beyond" where lived untold millions still untold; or by *death,* to be welcomed home to his mansion on high. In the meantime, he would bathe in God's limitless love. He prayed that all God's people might do the same.

He prayed that we might know the *breadth of God's love.* There is nothing narrow about God's love for people. Jesus loved the publicans and sinners. He loved the wayward prodigal, and He loved his bitter older brother. He loved Judas as much as He loved John. He loved Pilate as much as Peter, Annas and Antipas as much as Andrew and Ananias. Such is God's love. It is wonderfully wide. God loves the world, John tells us (John 3:16).

Paul prayed that we might know the *length of God's love.* How long does God love us? When, for instance, did God *start* loving us? Was it when we were saved? Was it when we first responded to the Holy Spirit's call? Was it when we were born? Was it when He saw us "in Adam"? Was it when He made the world? Was it when He decided, before the foundation of the world, to act in creation and, subsequently, to act in redemption? No, He loved us long before that. His is an everlasting love, a love without a beginning, as eternal as He Himself is.

When will God *stop* loving us? Is it when we disobey Him, perhaps, or when we fall into sin? Is it if we keep on sinning? In that case, will He allow us to plead for forgiveness only seven times seventy times? Has He stopped loving the lost in the black eternal darkness of endless night? No! But for them it is His holiness that must rule in equal force with His love.

Paul prayed, too, that we might know the *depth of God's love.* How deep is that love? Well, Jesus stepped off the throne of the universe and came to earth. He came from glory to Galilee, from Galilee to Gethsemane, from Gethsemane to Gabbatha, from Gabbatha to Golgotha, and from Golgotha to the grave. *That* was a long way down.

In the old days, when a sailing ship crept around the world, it had to keep close to the shore. A linesman would stand in the bow of the boat and cast a weighted line into the sea. He would report his findings on how deep or how shallow the water was beneath the keel. The best word was: "No bottom with this line." Such is the love of Christ: "No bottom!" All our sounding lines are far too short to measure the depths to which He was willing to go and the unfathomable depths of His love—for us.

Finally, Paul prayed that God's people might know the *height of God's love.* Jesus has now ascended on high and is seated in the highest heaven. His throne is high and lifted up. He reigns amidst scenes of splendor. Angel hosts bow down to Him. Bright, sinless beings rush to do His will. He basks in His Father's love. Has He now forgotten us? Oh, no! He has seated us with Himself in the heavenlies. Such is His love.

> How good is the God we adore,
> Our faithful unchangeable Friend!
> His love is as great as His power,
> And knows neither measure nor end![1]

1. Joseph Hart, "How Good Is the God We Adore," 1759.

Devotion 64

First Thessalonians

1 Thessalonians 1:8–10

Paul had barely founded the church at Thessalonica when he was forced to leave because of persecution. He left behind a church composed of babes in Christ. Paul made his way to Corinth; and from there, he wrote his first letter to these infant believers. To spur them on to growth and godliness, he wrote to them primarily of the second coming of Christ. Each of the five chapters in this epistle mentions it.

In chapter 1 Paul speaks of *a coming day*: "Ye turned to God from idols . . . and to wait for his Son from heaven, . . . even Jesus, which delivered us from the wrath to come" (vv. 9–10). Waiting! The idea is best illustrated in the marriage customs of the Jews in Bible times. First came the betrothal. The prospective bridegroom left his father's house and came to where the awaiting bride lived. There he negotiated a marriage covenant and paid the purchase price. Once the price was paid, the covenant went into effect. The couple was virtually regarded as man and wife, and the bride was regarded as set apart for her groom. The betrothal was ratified by the bride and groom drinking from a cup of wine. All this Jesus has done for us already.

After establishing the marriage covenant, the groom returned home where he remained for a year. During this time, both bride and groom prepared for the coming wedding. At length the day came, and the bridegroom came to take his bride to live with him. The bride expected him but did not know the exact time of his arrival. His coming was announced by a shout.

Next, Paul speaks of *a coronation day*: "For what is our hope, or joy, or crown of rejoicing? Are not even ye in the presence of our Lord Jesus Christ at his coming?" (2:19). Paul sees himself at the judgment seat of Christ, overwhelmed with bliss as he sees his beloved converts beaming at him in glory. They are the guarantee of his crown.

Then he tells them of *a confirmation day*: "To the end he may establish your hearts unblameable in holiness before God, even our Father, at the coming of our Lord Jesus Christ with all his saints" (3:13). The Holy Spirit is already at work in our hearts, seeking to make us more like Jesus. That work will be completed in a flash when Jesus comes. "We shall be like him; for we shall see him as he is," John says (I John 3:2). We shall take our place with all His saints at His coming. That will be the confirmation of the glorious fact that we belong to Him.

Up ahead is *a consummation day*: "The Lord himself shall descend from heaven with a shout, . . . the dead in Christ shall rise first: then we which are alive and remain shall be caught up . . . to meet the Lord in the air: and so shall we ever be with the Lord" (I Thess. 4:16–17). Let us continue the analogy of a Jewish wedding. The arrival of the bride was heralded with a shout. The groom received his bride, and the couple, with their companions, returned to his father's house. Just so, the Lord receives His church and takes her to glory. By the time the Jewish bride and groom are thus escorted home, the wedding guests are all assembled. The bride, heavily veiled, in the company of the groom, is escorted to the bridal chamber. They retire into seclusion. Once the consummation is announced, the feast begins and lasts for seven days.

Likewise we shall arrive home. The Old Testament saints will be gathered to welcome us home. The spiritual union of Christ and His church will be proclaimed. The marriage supper will take place in heaven while the final seven-year period of trouble and tribulation works out its course on earth.

Devotion 65

THE DEAD SHALL RISE FIRST

1 THESSALONIANS 4:16

"The dead in Christ *shall* rise first," God says. That is fair. These are the saints of God who hoped and prayed that the Lord would come while they were still alive, but death came instead. But they have this advantage over those who are alive and remain when Christ comes: they will go up first. "Then we which are alive and remain *shall* be caught up" (I Thess. 4:17). Those who are thus raptured will shout, "O death, where is thy sting?" Those who come bounding from their graves will sing, "O grave, where is thy victory?" (I Cor. 15:55). There is no room for doubt. "They *shall!*" God says. It was all settled in heaven a long time ago. The graves will be plundered of those who are asleep. The globe will be plundered of those who are alive. And the time is drawing nigh.

Imagine examining a little music box. When the lid is opened, the music box plays a little tune—"Raindrops Keep Falling on My Head." The box can be opened. Inside there is a small brass cylinder. That cylinder has a lot of little spikes sticking up all over it. Along with the cylinder and its spikes, there are a number of prongs. Those prongs make the various notes as the rotating spikes on the cylinder hit them.

Now, in a sense, when one looks inside that music box, he or she can see the whole tune. It is all pegged out, so to speak. But in order to *experience* the tune, it is necessary to wait for the process of time to run its course. One has to wait for the slow turning of the cylinder and for all the little spikes to hit all the corresponding prongs. As the cylinder slowly revolves, the music comes—

Ping! Ping! Ping-a-ping-a-ping!

That is how it is with us and with God. God sees the whole thing—the whole future, so to speak, is all pegged out in heaven. But we are creatures of time. We have to wait for the slow day-by-day process whereby the timeless purposes of God are wrought out in human history and experience.

But God, who is omniscient, sees everything, hears everything, and knows everything. It is all pegged out in heaven, and it will all be played out on earth. Those spokes will hit the corresponding prongs. The whole tune will be played. The music has already begun. The "Shall!" "Shall!" of God's Word is even now coming to pass. A few more notes, and we'll be gone. The dead in Christ *shall* rise; we who are alive and remain *shall* be caught up. Nothing can stop it.

That must have been comforting news for the Thessalonian believers. Paul had not been able to stay long in their city. He had been driven out by persecution. He arrived at length in Athens, having sent Timothy back to Thessalonica for news of the infant church. Timothy returned with good news. The church was alive and well. However, some believers had died in the short interval between the expulsion of Paul and the arrival of Timothy. Had they missed the rapture?

"Oh no!" Paul said, "not a bit of it!" The contrary was true. All believers would rise to meet the Lord in the air—but the dead in Christ would take precedence. The dead in Christ would rise first. It was good news for all!

Devotion 66

The Mystery of Godliness

1 Timothy 3:16

Great is the mystery," said the inspired apostle. "God was manifest in the flesh." First, there was *a plan rooted in eternity.* The plan was made before ever time began, before ever the rustle of an angel's wing disturbed the silence of eternity. It was made before ever the "mystery of iniquity" raised its head in the universe and before "the mystery of godliness" was conceived. It was the great plan of God to make guilty people godly. That plan was rooted in eternity. Thus Jesus is "the Lamb slain from [*before*] the foundation of the world" (Rev. 13:8).

Next, there was *a place rooted on earth.* God, in His wisdom, chose our planet to be the place where He would deal with the sin question when it raised its head in the universe. He would send His own Son to Earth, a tiny planet circling an insignificant sun, 30,000 light years from the center of a distant galaxy of 100 billion stars. And having chosen this planet to be the place, He picked a remote and insignificant town in a small and unimportant province to be the place. It was not glorious Athens, home of a thousand thinkers; not imperial Rome, home of countless legions; not favored Jerusalem; home of a long line of illustrious kings—but Bethlehem, hidden among the hills, away from the rush and roar of the world.

Then, too, there was *a path rooted in Scripture.* For once "the mystery" took form and God was manifest in flesh, He followed a predetermined path from a cradle, humble beyond anything that could have been imagined, to a death, horrendous, too, beyond anything imagined. And that predetermined path was spelled out in the library of thirty-nine Spirit-inspired books that made up the Old Testament. His birth, His life, His character, His death, His tomb, and His resurrection—everything was foreknown and foretold. No other person on this planet has had his coming character and career so amazingly foretold. When Herod heard from the wise men that the Messiah had been born, he appealed at once to the rabbis he kept at court—"And where is this one to be born?" he demanded. The answer came fast enough—"Bethlehem," they said. Bethlehem was to be the place where God would be manifest in flesh.

And so it was, for the Scripture cannot be broken. Herod, evil, guilt-ridden, crime-haunted man that he was, tried to murder the new-born Christ. He failed. So the mystery of making people godly had begun. And there is another part of the mystery, as penned by Giles Fletcher.

> A Child He was, and had not learned to speak
> Who with His words the world before did make;
> A mother's arms Him bare, He was so weak
> Who with His hands the vault of heaven could shake,
> See how small room my infant Lord doth take
> Whom all the world is not enough to hold.[1]

So the mystery of iniquity invaded our planet, brought by fallen Lucifer, hell's gift to earth. And now the mystery of godliness has come, brought by God the Son, no less—heaven's gift to us. And so we have to choose sides. Who but a fool would find it hard to decide which one to choose?

---

1. Cited by W. Robertson Nicoll, *The Incarnate Saviour* (Edinburgh: T. and T. Clark, 1899), 10.

Devotion 67

Enter into Rest

Hebrews 4:11

Years ago a missionary friend of mine was bumping along a backwoods African trail in a pickup truck. He saw a man up ahead, carrying a big bundle on his head. He stopped and asked the man if he'd like a ride. The man scrambled into the back of the pickup, and off they went. Presently, the missionary glanced in his rearview mirror and saw the man standing up, still holding the heavy load on his head. He stopped. "Why don't you put your load down?" he asked. "Oh," said the man, "I didn't know your truck could carry both me and my load!"

That reminds us of many Christians. They do not think that salvation includes putting down their load, whatever that load might be and however heavy it might be. They have not learned the lesson of Hebrews 4, that God loves to give rest to His own.

First, there is *creation rest.* "God . . . rested," we read, "on the seventh day" (Gen. 2:2). With a rush and a roar, the universe sprang into being. Astronomers set before us the picture of countless stars and their satellites traveling at inconceivable velocities, on prodigious orbits, with nearly inexhaustible reservoirs of energy. But it was God who flung these vast galactic empires into space. He summoned the light to shine and made the darkness to flee. He separated the waters. He raised the continents. He brought forth life in a myriad of forms. He crowned all this activity with the creation of human beings, male and female.

Then He rested. It was not because He was tired. He never gets tired. It took just ten words in Genesis 1:1 to record the original creative act. The brevity of the narrative matches the economy with which omnipotence expends its power. So God rested, not because He was tired, but because the work was done!

Then there is *Canaan rest.* "They shall not enter into my rest" (Heb. 3:11). That was God's verdict upon Israel at Kadesh-Barnea. He had brought them out. He had brought them through. Now He wanted to bring them in. There before them was the Promised Land. But by this time, the Hebrews had heard of the giants; and they dug in their heels. "Take us back to Egypt," they said. "We'd be better off there." So for forty long years, until all that doubting generation was dead, God caused them to roam the wilderness. They had trusted God to bring them out, but they doubted that God could bring them in. How sad! That generation never experienced Canaan rest.

Then, there is *covenant rest*: "For he spake in a certain place of the seventh day on this wise, And God did rest the seventh day from all his works" (Heb. 4:4). The Sabbath was an essential part of the Mosaic covenant. At Sinai God determined to share His own Sabbath rest with His blood-bought people. On the seventh day of each week, the people could turn aside from the daily concerns of the workaday world to enjoy fellowship with God. God deemed this weekly Sabbath rest so important that He appended the death sentence to it for those who desecrated it. We know all too well what happened. The rabbis so meddled with the Sabbath that it became a burden rather than a blessing, and God ended up abolishing the whole thing.

Now we have *Calvary rest*: "There remaineth therefore a rest to the people of God" (Heb. 4:9). Our rest is not in a day but in a deliverance, not in a weekly Sabbath but in God's wonderful Son. When He had finished the work God gave Him to do, He cried, "It is finished!" And so it is. Done is the work that saves.

As one of his great gospel crusades came to an end, D. L. Moody was accosted by a belated seeker. Already work crews were carting off the chairs and demolishing the platform. "Mr. Moody," said the late enquirer, "what must I do to be saved?" "You're too late," the evangelist replied. "Surely I'm not too late," the man said. "Oh yes," said Mr. Moody, "you're too late. You're two thousand years too late. If you want to do something, you're too late. It's all been done!" And he pointed the man to Christ and to Calvary rest. As the hymn says,

> My Savior, Thou hast offered rest,
> Oh, give it then to me;
> The rest of ceasing from myself
> To find my all in Thee.[1]

---

1. Evan Hopkins, "Oh, Give Me Rest from Self!"

Devotion 68

An All-Powerful High Priest

Hebrews 7:1–17

The Lord Jesus is introduced to us as a "high priest after the order of Melchisedec" (Heb. 5:10). For, like the Old Testament Melchizedek, He is both a *priest* and a *king*—something no priest of Aaron's line could ever be.

Hebrews 7:1–2 puts the emphasis on the *kingly* aspect of the Melchizedek priesthood: "For this Melchisedec," says the Holy Spirit, "[was] *king* of Salem, priest of the most high God . . . being by interpretation *King* of righteousness, and after that also *King* of Salem, which is *King* of peace." The title is repeated four times—King! King! King! King!

We read of Abraham's encounter with Priest-King Melchizedek in Genesis 14. Abraham had just won a military victory over a vastly superior force—a coalition of kings who, after devastating the Sodomites and their allies, were returning home laden with the spoils of war and with many captives. Abraham's nephew, Lot, and his family were among those captives. With a mere handful of men Abraham launched a night attack, surprised the invaders, put them to flight, and recovered the spoil and the captives.

Abraham suddenly had become the most powerful man in Canaan. He could have dictated whatever terms he liked to the neighboring chieftains. Instead, he turned his back on it all, realizing he was a pilgrim and a stranger on earth.

It was then that Abraham met Melchizedek, one who was able to bestow upon the pilgrim patriarch the true riches of righteousness and peace. The Canaanite chieftains in the area did not seem to know the value of a man like Melchizedek. Abraham did. Melchizedek was an Old Testament type of Christ, a man in touch with God, and Abraham instantly recognized his worth. Far from triumph going to Abraham's head, it brought him humbly to Melchizedek's feet. Nowhere does Abraham's spiritual stature show better than here.

The triumph gives way to the *table,* for Abraham at once took his place as a guest at Melchizedek's table. Bread and wine were on that table—symbols of the Lord's passion. The bread and the wine pointed forward to the coming One whose body would be broken and whose blood would be shed.

Then came the *title,* for at the table of Melchizedek Abraham learned a new name for God. He is "the most High God, possessor of heaven and earth" (Gen. 14:19). All the riches of the earth and all the resources of heaven were in His hand. No wonder Abraham could afford to take a carefree attitude toward material things. The "God Most High" was his God.

Now comes the *test.* The King of Sodom came with his offer of a deal. "You take the spoils," he said, "and I'll take the souls." Abraham did not even have to think. He wanted nothing to do with Sodom, its goods, or its king. Abraham loathed Sodom and all it stood for. The Possessor of heaven and earth was his God. What need had he of spoils of war or Sodom's gold? "I'll not have you say that you made Abraham rich," he said to Sodom's king. This spiritual victory stemmed from Abraham's recognition of Melchizedek as his own king-priest.

Today we are better off than Abraham by far for when all is said and done, Melchizedek was only a *type* of Christ. We have Christ Himself, a powerful Priest enthroned in heaven as God Most High and the Possessor of heaven and earth. What more could we want than that?

Devotion 69

Such an High Priest

Hebrews 8:1

When an Old Testament sinner came to the altar with his offering, it was up to the priest to guide him through the various rituals specified for the particular kind of offering being brought.

It might be a sin offering, for instance. The sinner would be required to lay his hand upon the sacrifice. Then he must take the proffered knife and personally slay the lamb. The priest would then dismember it and examine it. If it passed the test, he would place it on the fire, and the sinner would see it burned to ashes in his stead. He would go away feeling much better about his sin.

Before long, however, he might have doubts. He would go back to the priest. "Do you know," he might say, "I really don't feel any different than I did before? Are you sure that the blood of that animal really took away my sin?" The priest would say, "I suppose so. At least, the Law prescribes such and such a sacrifice for such and such a sin. I cannot tell you any more than that." It was all very unsatisfactory. The New Testament underlines the point. The book of Hebrews says, "It is not possible that the blood of bulls and of goats should take away sins" (10:4). As the hymn writer says:

> Not all the blood of beasts
> On Jewish altars slain
> Could give the guilty conscience peace
> Nor wash away the stain.[1]

Some years ago I was in Vichy in France. It is a busy spa health resort to which people come from all over the world to take the cure. Brooding over the town is the Roman Catholic Church of Our Lady of Healing, where a black statue of Mary dominates all. It was the dome,

---

1. Isaac Watts, "Not All the Blood of Beasts," 1709.

however, that most impressed me. High up in the dome is a picture. In that picture Christ is in the shadows, and Mary fills the foreground. The picture is so painted that Mary's robe lights up when the sun shines on it. She stands triumphant, trampling a writhing serpent. On the base of the dome are two quotations. One reads: "God so loved the world He gave His only Son" (a quotation from John 3:16). The other one, executed in letters that dwarf the Bible text, gives a quotation from Saint Bernard: "It is God's will that we obtain all things through Mary!" That painting struck me forcibly with the realization that the Virgin Mary is Rome's great mediator, not Christ.

A moment's thought, however, shows the fallacy of that. All over the world, at any given moment, thousands of devout Catholics are praying to Mary. She is bombarded with countless prayers in thousands of tongues. To hear them all, she would need to be *omnipresent.* To unravel them all, and be cognizant of them all, she would need to be *omniscient.* To respond to them all, she would need to be *omnipotent.* "If you want anything," says Rome, "then go to Mary." But Mary is not God. She has none of the attributes of deity. So why pray to Mary? It is not very satisfactory, we might well say.

We need not a Mary, nor a fallible priest, whether of Rome or anywhere else. We need a priest who is "able also to save them to the uttermost that come unto God by him," a priest who "ever liveth to make intercession" (Heb. 7:25).

Thankfully we have "such an high priest" (Heb. 8:1). He is our Mediator with the Father (1 Tim. 2:5). He is all we need. He is a *powerful* High Priest, for in the tradition of Melchizedek (Gen. 14:18–20; Heb. 6:20), He is both Priest and King. He is a *permanent* High Priest, for He is alive forevermore and has the keys of death and hades (Rev 1:18). He is a *perfect* High Priest, free from all sin and able to deal with ours (Heb 9:7, 11–14). And He is a *patient* High Priest, "touched with the feeling of our infirmities" (Heb 4:15), being both God and Man and therefore able to make intercession for us. He is very satisfactory indeed!

Devotion 70

The Blood of Jesus

Hebrews 10:19

The book of Hebrews tells of blood that "speaketh better things than that of Abel" (Heb. 12:24). Abel's blood cried aloud for *punishment.* The blood of Jesus cries aloud for *pardon.*

Blood is unique in the complex chemistry of life. There are other fluids in the body—saliva, tears, gastric juices, and so on. But these are all *products* of the body. Blood is a *part* of the body—just as hands and hair are parts of the body. It contains both red and white cells and is constantly in motion. Each of the billions of red blood cells in the body live for about 120 days, then dies and is replaced.

The chemistry of blood is extremely complex. Hemoglobin, alone, is made up of thousands of atoms of carbon, hydrogen, nitrogen, iron, oxygen, and sulfur. Each of these atoms has to be hooked up to its neighbor atoms in exactly the right way. Such a substance couldn't just "happen."

Nowadays we classify blood by types. Before a blood transfusion can take place, the blood types of donor and recipient must match. Scientists now think that each person's blood type is as separate and distinctive from all others as are one's fingerprints. Such is *human* blood, the life stream of the body, awesome in its function and its form.

Now think of Jesus and *His* blood, for His blood was even more distinctive than ours. The blood of Jesus was unique. No such blood ever flowed in other human veins. Our blood is tainted by sin, but His never was. His blood was immaculate. The essential fact of the Lord's birth is that He was virgin born. He had a human mother but no human father. Instead, the Holy Spirit came upon Mary; and the power of the Highest overshadowed her, ensuring that His blood, the blood of Jesus, was kept from contamination. Here is the important point—*the blood that flows in the arteries of a babe, developing in its mother's womb, is not derived from its mother. The baby's blood is its own blood, produced within the body of the developing embryo. It is only after an embryo has been impregnated that it begins to develop blood. Every drop of a baby's blood is developed by the embryo itself.* Since a baby in its mother's womb may have a different blood type altogether than its mother, the body sees to it that not one drop of blood ever passes from the mother to the child.

Jesus was virgin born. That means He had no drop of Joseph's blood in His veins and no drop of His mother's blood either. The blood that flowed in His veins was unique blood created by the direct action of the overshadowing Holy Spirit. It was *sinless blood.* It was *shed blood.* It is *saving blood.* And now, the Holy Spirit tell us, it is *speaking blood.* Abel's blood spoke, and God could hear it. It demanded vengeance. It cried for retribution. It cried aloud for retribution; it cried aloud from the dust of the earth. Cain the murderer became a stranger and a vagabond on the earth, haunted by the voice of his brother's blood.

The precious blood of Christ cries aloud too, for it too was shed by wicked people. It cries not for retribution, but for our redemption; and it cries not from the ground but from glory, from the mercy seat above.

On the annual Day of Atonement, the high priest took the blood of the sacrifice into the Holy of Holies and sprinkled it on the mercy seat. The types of the Old Testament are as accurate as mathematics. What was done symbolically with the blood of the sacrifice has been done likewise with the blood of Christ. He took it to heaven and placed it on the true mercy seat (Heb. 9:11–28).

> O! precious is the flow
> That washes white as snow;
> No other fount I know,
> *Nothing but the blood of Jesus.*[1]

---

1. Robert Lowry, "Nothing But the Blood," 1876.

Devotion 71

Boldness to Enter

Hebrews 10:19–20

For some fifteen hundred years the veil had hung between the Holy Place and the Holy of Holies in the tabernacle and then the temple in Jerusalem. It served one purpose—to keep people out of the presence of God. It was death to go beyond that veil. Indeed, it was death for anyone not born into the family of Aaron to go anywhere near the veil. Calvary changed all that. The veil was rent when Jesus died, and believers are now invited to come boldly right into the presence of God.

Let us get the full impact of that. Picture an Old Testament Moabite finding his way to the gate of the tabernacle and there being stopped by the keeper of the gate. The conversation might go something like this:

Keeper: Who are you?

Moabite: I'm a man from Moab. I have heard about your God. I should like to go in there and worship Him.

Keeper: You can't do that. The Law of our God bans a Moabite from the worship of God until his tenth generation.

Moabite: What would I have to do to escape this curse of the Law of your God?

Keeper: You would have to be born again. You would have to be born an Israelite, be born of one of the tribes of Dan, shall we say, or Ephraim or Judah.

Moabite: I wish I'd been born an Israelite, of the tribe of Judah. I would go in and help those people who are serving the altar. I could help them carry away the ashes, perhaps, or help them move the tabernacle when you people march on from place to place.

Keeper: Oh, no! You couldn't do that. You would need to be born a Levite, for only people of the tribe of Levi can touch those things.

Moabite: I wish I had been born an Israelite, of the tribe of Levi. What I should really like to do is help those robed priests with their work with sacrifices at the altar there. I could help lift those heavy animals onto the altar, perhaps.

Keeper: No, you could not do that. You would have to be born not only of the tribe of Levi but also of the family of Aaron. Only Aaron's sons can be priests.

Moabite: I wish I had been born an Israelite, of the tribe of Levi, and a priest of the family of Aaron. I should like to go in there, into that covered shrine yonder. I see priests going in and out of there at times. Tell me, what is it like in there?

Keeper: It is very beautiful in there, gleaming with gold, rich color, and costly linen. There is a golden table in there, a golden lampstand and a golden altar. Then there is a veil, thick, costly, and beautiful. Beyond that veil is what we call "the Holy of Holies." It contains the ark of the covenant, with its mercy seat. You can see that cloudy pillar that overshadows the camp of Israel. You see how it rests upon the tabernacle? God dwells in that cloud. It not only overshadows God's people, but it actually sits upon the mercy seat upon the ark.

Moabite: Oh, that I had been born a priest of the family of Aaron. I would love to go beyond the veil and worship your God in that holy, holy place.

Keeper: Oh, no. You couldn't do that. Only the high priest can go in there. You would need to be born of the house of Eleazar of the family of Aaron, of the tribe of Levi, and of the nation of Israel before ever you could even think of going in there. God's high priests come from the house of Eleazar.

Moabite: I wish I had been born an Israelite, of the tribe of Levi, of the family of Aaron, and of the house of Eleazer. I would go in there again and again. I would go in three times a day. I would stay long hours in there worshiping your God.

Keeper: Oh no! Even the high priest can go in there only once a year, on the Day of Atonement. Even then, he can enter

> only after taking the most elaborate ritual precautions. Moreover, he cannot tarry in there. He must present the blood of the sacrifice before the mercy seat and then hurry out again. So you see, Mr. Moabite, you have no hope whatsoever of entering "inside the veil."

We see the Moabite turn away sadly.

But that was *before Calvary*. When Jesus died, God tore the veil in two (Matt. 27:51). Now He invites all believers to come in. We are to have boldness to "enter into the holiest by the blood of Jesus" (Heb. 10:19). We can come as often as we like, we can stay as long as we like, and we can talk to Him about whatever we like. It is a miracle of grace. God has given us this priceless privilege. It should fill our hearts with wonder, love, and praise. It should move us to spend much time in there, where Jesus sits enthroned.

Devotion 72

By Faith We Understand

Part 1

Hebrews 11:3

Hebrews 11 is the picture gallery of faith. A host of Old Testament giants are portrayed in this chapter. We meet Abel and Enoch, Noah and Abraham, Isaac and Jacob, all people whose faith turned them into giants. But the list begins with *us!* "Through faith *we*," the sacred writer says. "Through faith *we* understand that the worlds were framed by the word of God." There is an alternate translation ("through faith we understand that the ages were formed by the word of God"), but for now we shall let the statement stand as it is.

We gaze about us at globes and galaxies, and we stand in awe at the word of God that spoke them into being. The meaning of the text as found in the Authorized Version is obvious enough. God's word brought into existence the great empires of space.

Let us take our own star, the sun, as an example. It is 93 million miles away from us (a distance equivalent to more than 18,000 round trips between San Francisco and New York). It has a diameter of 864,000 miles, about 109 times that of the earth. The temperature of the sun's interior is about 27 million degrees Fahrenheit.

The sun is the center of a solar system. That solar system consists of the sun; eight planets; and numerous moons, asteroids, and comets. After the moon, Earth's closest neighbors in space are Mercury, Venus, and Mars. Pluto, no longer considered a planet, is at the outer edge of the solar system. So great is the sun's gravitational sway that its influence extends to a distance a thousand times farther than the orbit of Pluto before its power begins to be canceled by the pull of other stars.

All this was framed by the word of God. But our sun, solar system, and sphere are only a puny part of the story. Our sun is one star, and a moderate star at that, in a galaxy of 100 billion stars. We call that galaxy the Milky Way. It has a diameter of 100,000 light years—an inconceivable 600 million billion miles. The sun is located 30,000 light years from the hub of the galaxy which it orbits once every 225 million years.

But there are 100 billion other galaxies in known space besides our own. Some of them are receding from us at speeds close to the speed of light (186,000 miles per second). All this was framed by the word of God.

Outer space is full of wonders. The great Orion Nebula, for instance, is a vast cradle for the birth of new stars. It has enough raw material for 10,000 stars the size of our sun. More than fifty percent of all stars are binaries, two stars moving through space together. Sometimes a star known as a supernova explodes. When that occurs, a compressed core remains. We call it a neutron star. A *pinhead's* worth of neutron star material weights about *a million tons!*

And so it goes, on and on, a vast, fascinating universe of worlds made by the word of God. The Word of God says so. And God cannot lie. What words! What worlds!

Devotion 73

By Faith We Understand

Part 2

Hebrews 11:3

Through faith we understand that the worlds were framed by the word of God." The surface meaning draws our attention to the great *empire of space.* Beyond our own small globe, beyond a hundred billion galaxies, before the beginning of time, is God in all His omnipotent power, putting forth His word and bringing it all into being. Faith accepts that to be so.

Some, however, see a different picture here. The word for "worlds" is *aionas,* which literally means "ages." If rendered that way then, of course, the verse tells us that the ages, the various *epochs of time,* were framed by the word of God. In this case, our understanding is directed not to God's activity in *creation* but to His activity in *redemption.* Faith soars, not only at the omnipotence of God in making the heavens but also at the omniscience of God in making history. We see God pursuing His grand purposes in the redemption of Adam's ruined race being carried forward age after age. Page after page of the Word of God reveals this governing activity of God in the onward march of human affairs. A correct understanding of God's plans and purposes in dealing thus with the human race in different ways and at difficult times is essential to a proper understanding of the Word of God itself.

First, there was *the age of innocence* when Adam and Eve lived in the garden of Eden under ideal conditions. That age ended with the fall and with the banishment of Adam and Eve from Paradise.

Next came *the age of conscience.* A knowledge of right and wrong was the one legacy the human race inherited from the fall. This age also ended in judgment. Humanity became so wicked that God purged the earth with the flood.

Then came *the age of government.* The sword of the magistrate was given to Noah, and the death penalty was instituted as a deterrent to high crime. But a descendant of Ham named Nimrod converted the sword of the magistrate into the sword of the conqueror, turned it against others, and tried to found a global society. The building of the Tower of Babel was the final expression of all this godless humanism, materialism, and rebellion against God's word. Judgment followed.

The age of promise came next. God began again, this time with an individual. To Abraham He gave many great and precious promises, including possession of the land of Canaan and all the territory between the Nile and the Euphrates. The Promised Land seemed a remote possession, however, when the heirs of the promises found themselves in Egyptian bondage and facing total annihilation. Then Moses came to be their kinsman-redeemer and this nation of several million slaves was set free and headed for home—the Promised Land. The speed with which the emancipated Hebrews, on their way from Egypt to Canaan, turned from God to idols, is eloquent. In Egypt they had learned that a sacred cow was one of Egypt's many gods. The swift acceptance by the Hebrews of Aaron's golden calf shows clearly that they were attracted to Egyptian idolatry. Their various apostasies in the wilderness on the way to Canaan exposed them to judgment and great peril.

Next came *the age of law.* Moses, having emancipated the enslaved Hebrews, gave them God's Law and brought the people to the borders of the Promised Land. The Mosaic Law, given at Sinai, was summed up in ten basic commandments (Exod. 20). It was expanded in the Pentateuch to 613 commandments covering all aspects of life. This age lasted through the days of the theocracy, the monarchy, and the dependency. It ended when God set Israel aside for the rejection of Christ and put an end to Judaism as a religion He could bless.

Then followed *the age of grace* (the church age). During this long period God has been calling out a people and baptizing them into the church, the mystical body of Christ.

This age will be followed by *the age of wrath.* God will rapture His church and then pour out His wrath upon Israel and the nations.

Then will come *the millennial age,* during which Christ will reign on earth in power and glory.

Finally, *the ages to come* will be inaugurated by the creation of a new heaven and a new earth.

Thus, God sovereignly tests human beings under various conditions. It was not that God had any need to experiment in hope of finding a system that would work. The purpose of all these changes in God's handling of human affairs was to prove to His fallen creatures how utterly sinful and fallen they are and how completely dependent on God they are for salvation and everlasting life.

Devotion 74

By Faith Noah

HEBREWS 11:7

At last! The work was done. The great carpenter of the Old Testament had finished the work God had given him to do. A judgment-proof means of salvation had been provided for all, and at unknown but enormous cost. Giant trees had been felled, vast timbers had been hewn, and hauled, and hammered into place. All had proceeded according to plan. A blueprint for salvation, thought out in heaven, had been wrought out on earth.

The work had been vast. Blood and sweat and tears and toil had been the toll. But now the roof was on. Stalls and rooms and storage bins were all in place. All had been done according to plan.

Now came *the last activity*. The ark had to be made leak-proof, safe, and secure against sea and storm, howling wind, and heaving wave. So pitch was prepared and applied, inside and out, over every inch of the surface of the ark, into every nook and cranny.

In terms of the type, it is significant that the Hebrew word for "pitch" comes from the same word the word "atonement" comes from. It means "to cover." The pitch kept the judgment waters of the flood out of the ark. Similarly, atonement keeps the judgment out of the soul.

The pitch was lavishly applied. Then cautious Noah, pitch pot in one hand, brush in the other, inspected the ark one more time. It was done. It had been an enormous work. The ark, when finished, was the shape of a coffin. It would take those who trusted God through death to a new life in a new world.

Then came *the last appeal*. Methuselah died. His longevity had become a legend even in an age when people lived a long, long time. His father, Enoch, had been a patriarch, a preacher, and a prophet. He foretold the second coming of Christ and, nearer to his own age, the impending judgment of the flood. He even set a date for it. "When he dies it shall come" was the prophetic name he gave to his son. And now Methuselah was dead. Probably Noah, a preacher of righteousness, preached Methuselah's funeral. "He is dead!" We can almost hear him cry, "It will come! The heavens will tear asunder. The storm is about to burst. Flee from the wrath to come. Salvation can be yours in the ark." But he preached in vain, his last sermon no more productive than his first one. He had preached for a hundred twenty years, all the time the ark was being built—in vain! People thought he was a fool.

Then came *the last animal*; in twos and in sevens the animals came. Big and small, wild and tame, an endless line of them came, until at last the final creature found its place on board. This parade of beasts and birds must have been an astonishing testimony to the godless people of earth. Still, they shrugged it off as some kind of conjurer's trick. "Very clever! Great circus act! Wonder how he did it!" they would say.

Finally came *the last act*. Noah and his family, just eight people, went on board the ark. There was a last look around, a final call to some wavering person, a last glimpse of the cloudless sky! And the door was shut, and a week later the storm burst.

But Noah was saved. His wife was saved. Shem, Ham, and Japheth were saved. Their wives were saved. Fear and faith went hand in hand. But Noah's faith had saved his family. What peace that must have brought to his soul. Happy indeed are the godly parents who live to see their children all safely in the ark.

Devotion 75

By Faith Sarah

Hebrews 11:11

Oh but she wanted a son! It was a common enough desire. Every devout woman in the Word, from Sarah to Elizabeth, longed for a son. It was a joyous occasion to be married. The birth of a girl was a joyful occasion. But to give birth to a boy was the crown of joy for a Hebrew maid, for perhaps her son might turn out to be His Son, the long promised Seed of the woman, no less, the Savior of mankind.

So we come back to Sarah and *her longing*. For Sarah had no son. Ishmael did not count, though once she had imagined Abraham and Hagar could give her a surrogate son. The boy born of that union gave her nothing but grief. In the end, both Hagar and Ishmael had to be cast out. The whole thing had been a disaster.

So Sarah longed for a son. Above all else in this world, she wanted a son. She had everything else. Abraham was rich. He had flocks, and herds, and tents, and camels, and servants born in his house. And he was strong. The Canaanite tribes feared him. He was a mighty prince among them. But for all his wealth and power, he could not buy Sarah a son. She was barren.

Which brings us to *her laugh*. Abraham settled down at Hebron in the Promised Land. One day he was sitting in the door of his tent; and Sarah was within, inside the veil. Three mysterious visitors appeared, walking toward his tent. Abraham knew well enough who they were. One was God the Son. The other two were angels, Gabriel and Michael perhaps. They dined at Abraham's table. They paused. They had words for him before they went their way. Curiosity got the better of Sarah. She crept up to the partition to hear what was being said. "Within a year Sarah will have a son," the spokesman said (Gen. 18:10). Sarah burst out laughing. It was too funny for words! She was ninety, and Abraham was a hundred! No wonder Sarah laughed (v. 12).

Then comes *her lie.* "Why did Sarah laugh?" God said. "Is any thing too hard for the Lord?" (Gen. 18:14). Frightened, Sarah lied. "I laughed not," she said (v. 15). Imagine lying in the face of God Himself. Yet all God did was contradict her and correct her and leave it at that. Such is His grace. It is a good thing God does not mark and punish all our sins. If He did, He would soon depopulate the globe.

This brings us to *her logic.* Hebrews 11 says, "She judged him faithful who had promised." She stopped laughing and doubting and became as great a believer as Abraham. She fixed her eyes on God. For the next year she looked for a son. Someone might say: "Maybe it will abort, you are so old." "*No!*" she would say. "Maybe it will be a girl." "*No!*" she would say. "Maybe you'll die; you are so old." "*No!* Please stop making silly remarks," she would say, "or I'll start laughing again—for sheer joy. *God* has promised me *a son,* and a son I shall have. Indeed, God has already named him—*Isaac* ["laughter"] is his name."

Such was her logic. God had promised. What more could anyone want than that? So let us laugh at our doubts and at the difficulties in the way. God's promises are sure. They are backed by all the resources of His deity. What more, indeed, could we want than that?

Devotion 76

By Faith Rahab

Hebrews 11:31

Rahab's faith was extraordinary. It not only saved her soul, but it also put her in the royal family and made her an ancestress of Christ. The former Jericho harlot is listed in the picture gallery of faith, along with such worthies as Enoch, Noah, Abraham, Isaac, Jacob, David, and Samuel. But her spiritual pilgrimage did not begin with faith, by any means, though she was eager enough to seize hold of salvation the moment the opportunity arose.

We are to think, first, of her *fear*. The Old Testament narrative tells of the coming of the two Hebrews to her house. She knew at once they were spies, but that only loosened her tongue. She was terrified. All Jericho was terrified. The walls of Jericho were great and strong, but walls are only as strong as those who defend them. And the people of Jericho were in mortal fear of the foe that had suddenly come marching up from the skyline and now were encamped nearby.

There was good reason for that fear. A generation ago this same Hebrew people had overthrown and spoiled the land of Egypt. For some reason they had not invaded Canaan then, but everyone in Jericho expected them to invade Canaan now. The fear of the plagues of Egypt hung over Jericho. Rahab made no bones about it. It is not at all unusual for fear to come before faith. The work of conviction comes before the work of conversion.

We think next of her *falsehood*. She hid the two spies and shielded them from the king of Jericho's men. To do so, she had to tell a lie. The Holy Spirit records it but makes no comment. In fact, it is hard to see how she could have done anything else and still saved the spies, let alone her own life. In any case, it was a time of war; a different ethic prevails in war. Killing, for instance, is countenanced in war when the occasion requires. So is deception. Moreover, the Holy Spirit makes no fuss about Rahab's falsehood. He chose to overlook it. It was this pagan woman's way of showing whose side she was on.

Then comes her *faith*. Before lowering the spies to safety, Rahab talked to them about her deepest need. No one had to tell her she was a sinner. What she needed was a Savior. She was in peril, and she knew it. The spies gave her a pledge. She was to tie a scarlet cord in her window. It would be the token of her faith. She wasted no time. The moment the messengers of God were gone, that scarlet cord was in place.

Her trust was in that token. It symbolized the blood of the covenant by which she was sealed. She was safe. That scarlet line told her so, all outward appearances to the contrary notwithstanding. And the outward circumstances were ominous enough—the daily, eerie march of the somber Israelites, in utter silence, around the doomed city. But Rahab's faith never failed. She knew who she had believed and was persuaded that He was able to keep that which she'd committed unto Him against that day.

Finally, there was her *family*. Diligently she witnessed to them so that they too came and took shelter behind the scarlet cord. That was her old family. Not long after the fall of Jericho and her salvation, she had a new family. The people of God became her people too. She eagerly took to that family. Indeed, a man named Salmon, perhaps one of the two spies, married her (Matt. 1:5). As a result, she became an ancestress of David and a long line of kings and, above all, of Christ. Oh, for like precious faith!

Devotion 77

One Morsel of Meat

Hebrews 12:16

Esau, . . . for one morsel of meat sold his birthright." He is one of a large company, sad to say. *David* sold his for a short moment of passion. *Judas* sold his for a small margin of profit. *Peter* sold his at Antioch for a shallow murmur of praise. Esau sold out for a single bowl of stew. How cheaply we sell our eternal salvation or our eternal reward.

In his famous *Screwtape Letters,* C. S. Lewis gives us the Devil's formula for pleasure. The demon points out to his fellow demon, his pupil in the art of temptation, that although pleasure has its uses as a means of seduction and enslavement, it is a tricky tool to use because it was God who invented pleasure, not Satan. The best the Devil can do with pleasure is to distort it and persuade people to abuse it. Thus, he strives to develop in them a craving for pleasure so that he gets them hooked on it until they want more and more stimulation and get less and less satisfaction. The ultimate aim is to get a person's soul for nothing. Satan got Esau's cheaply enough. He got it for "one morsel of meat."

Esau and Jacob were twins. Esau was born ahead of Jacob by the narrowest of margins, so, as the older brother, he stood in line to receive the patriarchal blessing. That blessing carried with it certain property rights, patriarchal rights, and priestly rights. Esau, however, cared for none of those things. Jacob did. Jacob coveted them and determined to get them at all costs, forgetful of the fact that even before his birth God had already promised them to him.

Esau was a man of the world. He liked to hunt and fish and sit around with the boys. He was ambitious to get on in this world. He married unsaved women and carved out a position for himself among the Hittites. He had no interest in the things of God, even though his grandfather was Abraham. Doubtless Abraham had talked to him about his conversion, how he was looking for a city that had foundations, whose builder and maker was God. It all sounded like pie in the sky to Esau.

But not to Jacob. All his faults and failings notwithstanding, Jacob had his priorities right. If there was one thing he wanted, it was the blessing of God in his life. He had not yet learned, however, that you cannot get spiritual things by worldly and carnal means. So Jacob set out to get Esau's birthright, no matter what it took to get it. He caught Esau when he was tired and hungry and discouraged, and he dangled a bowl of stew before him and clinched the deal—Esau's spiritual birthright for one serving of stew.

Esau never changed. God called him a "profane person." Later Esau tried to get back with a dish of venison what he had sold for a bowl of stew but failed. He remained a profane person, a person who had no room for God, to the day of his death. That "one morsel of meat" was a costly morsel indeed. It was as expensive as the "sop" Jesus handed to Judas in the upper room on the eve of His betrayal. It was a morsel that sealed his doom. For no sooner had Judas eaten it than Satan entered into him, and all hell took over his soul.

Well might we beware lest we sell our souls for a serving of this world's pleasures.

Devotion 78

An Innumerable Company

Hebrews 12:22–23

"Ye are come," says Hebrews, "to an innumerable company of angels, to the general assembly and church of the firstborn." Here we have two vast populations and two different orders. There are those in heaven by right of *creation*, the heavenly native-born hosts; and there are those in heaven by right of *redemption*, the blood-bought human hosts.

Think first of the *heavenly hosts*. John tells us that there are ten thousand times ten thousand of them and thousands of thousands (Rev. 5:11). In other words, they are countless, a multitude that no one can number. Heaven is their home and holiness is the breath of their being. They are mentioned more than 100 times in the Old Testament and 165 times in the New.

There are *messenger* angels, such as Gabriel. There are *ministering* angels; "ministering spirits" is the way the Holy Spirit describes them (Heb. 1:14). As such they visited Abraham in his tent, delivered Lot from Sodom, escorted Jacob back to the Promised Land, and protected Jacob from Laban's spite. Then, too, there are *martial* angels, headed by Michael, the archangel. They are active in the wars of the Lord and in end-time events.

The rightful home of these exalted beings is in heaven, a land of fadeless day, where streets are paved with gold and walls are built of jasper, where they count not time by years, and where Christ sits on the right hand of the Majesty on high. What stories they will have to tell us when we arrive in heaven, stories of how, unknown to us, they ministered to our needs on our journey home.

But the Holy Spirit mentions another company in heaven, the *human hosts*, made up of men and women and boys and girls who have been washed in the blood of the Lamb and made fit for the holiness and happiness of heaven. He sees two such companies.

There is "the general assembly . . . of the firstborn" (Heb. 12:23). The word used is *paneguris*. It was used in classical Greek of a festive gathering. It appears to be employed here to describe a convocation convened in heaven to do honor to the saints of God, particularly to that special company of the redeemed who compose the bride of Christ.

In the Old Testament the firstborn of both people and beasts were to be set apart for God (Exod. 13:13, 15; 34:20). A firstborn son was to be redeemed. A firstborn clean beast was to be sacrificed. If the animal was unclean, it either had its neck broken or it was redeemed by a lamb. Later the tribe of Levi was chosen from among the tribes of Israel, and its members were substituted for the general firstborn (Num. 3:12, 41, 46; 8:13–19).

Special privileges accrued to the firstborn. To the firstborn son belonged the birthright, which included headship of the family, the right to be the family priest, and, in the early days, the right to be the progenitor of Christ. It also included a double portion of the Father's property.

Viewed in relation to the Gentile nations, God called Israel "My son, even *my* firstborn" (Exod. 4:22). Pharaoh was warned that if he refused to acknowledge this primacy among the nations of the Hebrew people, then God would slay *his* son, even his firstborn. And, even more mysterious and terrible was that God would single out all the firstborn Egyptian males and all the firstborn beasts in the barn and in the fields and slay them too (Exod. 11:5).

"The general assembly . . . of the firstborn" mentioned in Hebrews 12:23 are the Jewish friends of the bridegroom. Paul foresaw the day when, in the ages to come, God would show "the exceeding riches of his grace in his kindness toward us through Christ Jesus" (Eph. 2:7). The angels will marvel at this proof of God's grace. Saints of other ages will marvel too.

Closely linked with this general assembly of God's Old Testament firstborn ones is the "church of the firstborn, which are written in heaven" (Heb. 12:23). Here we have the raptured and ascended church, the bride of Christ, taking the highest place that heaven affords, and being seated with Christ far above all principalities and powers and every name that is named. "Rejoice," said Jesus to His disciples, "because your names are written in heaven" (Luke 10:20). Think of it! Our names are written there! That acknowledges us as children of God, as joint-heirs with

Christ, and as members of the aristocracy of heaven! "There!" David would have said, had such a truth been revealed to Him. "There, send *that* to the chief musician!" That is something to sing about down here, even as they sing about it over there.

Devotion 79

As . . .

1 Peter 2

Peter had learned from Jesus how to paint pictures with words. He specializes in the strategic use of similes. For example, in I Peter he says that we "were *as sheep going astray*" (2:25). It is astonishing how often the Bible likens people to animals, to wolves and dogs and sows. Jesus called Herod a fox. He likened Himself to a hen. We are all likened to sheep.

A sheep is not strong, and it is not swift, and it is not smart. It has a tendency to stray and put itself in peril. Moreover, a sheep that strays soon finds itself lost and with no ability to find its way back to the fold. Peter said that we, wayward sheep that we are, have "now returned." A sheep can be returned to the shepherd only if the shepherd seeks and finds it. That, then, is what happened, and what rejoicing that causes in heaven. As the hymn writer puts it:

> But all thro' the mountains thunder-riven,
> And up from the rocky steep,
> There arose a glad cry to the gate of heav'n,
> "Rejoice! I have found my sheep!"
> And the angels echoed around the throne,
> "Rejoice, for the Lord brings back His own."[1]

We were "*as newborn babes*" (2:2). The one characteristic of a newborn babe is its utter helplessness and obvious need. Therefore a local church is to be an incubator, not a refrigerator. Some churches are so cold, it is no wonder that they see no one saved. They remind us of the little girl who learned a text in Sunday school: "Many are called, but few are chosen." When asked to recite it, she said, "Many are cold and a few are frozen!" New converts need love and care; and when they get themselves

---

1. Elizabeth C. Clephane, "The Ninety and Nine," 1868.

in a mess, they need to be cleaned up. They need to be fed. We cannot expect babes in Christ to act like mature saints of God. We need to feed them "the sincere milk of the Word" so that they will grow in grace and increase in the knowledge of God.

We are "*as obedient children*" (1:14). Peter contrasts "the former lusts" with "the family likeness." Babes in Christ must be taught obedience to the Word of God. The Lord Jesus Himself "learned . . . obedience" (Heb. 5:8) and became "obedient unto death" (Phil. 2:8). Peter says, "It is written, Be ye holy; for I am holy" (I Peter 1:16). This Old Testament quotation is appended to a chapter that lists all the dietary "do's" and "don'ts" of the Law (Lev. 11). There is always the danger of thinking that we have discharged our religious obligations when we have conformed with some rule or ritual. God demands much more than that. He demands holiness.

Moreover, we are "*as strangers and pilgrims*" (I Peter 2:11). Cain described himself as a fugitive and a vagabond. By contrast, Abraham confessed himself to be a pilgrim and a stranger. The sons of Heth, however, said he was a mighty prince among them. Nobody ever said that of Lot, who gave up being a pilgrim and a stranger in order to get on in this world. A *stranger* is a person away from home. He is an alien and out of his environment. His looks, language, and likings are all different from those round about him. He is a citizen of another country. A *pilgrim* is more than a person away from home; he is going home. He has his mind set on a long-desired place. Our affections are to be set thus on things above, where Christ sits at the right hand of the Majesty on high. We're going home.

Finally, we are "*as [living] stones*" (2:5). The Lord once called Peter a pebble (*petros*) and Himself a rock (*petra*) (Matt. 16:18). Peter carries the simile over to all believers. We are to be living stones, hewed out of nature's dark mine, shaped and fashioned by the Holy Spirit, and fitted by God into that "habitation of God through the Spirit" He is now erecting for eternity (Eph. 2:22). When David Livingstone went to Africa, it was to evangelize, to explore, and to emancipate. When he died, a grieving nation followed his coffin to Westminster Abbey, where he was buried along with many of England's greats. One of the nation's most popular periodicals wrote his epitaph. It read: "Granite may crumble but this is living stone." Well may we strive so that some such epitaph might one day be ours.

Devotion 80

Peter and the Bomb

2 Peter 3:10–13

The atomic age burst upon the world with a rush and a roar at 8:15 in the morning on August 16, 1945, when the United States dropped the first atomic bomb on Hiroshima. The bomb exploded 1,800 feet above the city, and the city of some 350,000 was virtually leveled. Mankind now had in its hands an apocalyptic weapon of mass destruction.

It is an extraordinary fact that Simon Peter, an uneducated Galilean peasant, wrote down an accurate description of the nuclear age two thousand years ago. The background of this astonishing prophecy is one of growing skepticism and scorn for the things of God, especially for truth concerning the second coming of Christ (2 Peter 3:4). Scoffers fail to reckon on the fact that God's timetable is much more vast than ours. A thousand years with Him passes as swiftly as a twenty-four-hour day does with us.

Peter's prophecy, while not couched in scientific language, is amazingly accurate just the same. The Greek words he chooses are very precise words. "The heavens shall pass away with a great noise," he says, "and the elements shall melt with fervent heat, the earth also and the works that are therein shall be burned up . . . all these things shall be dissolved" (2 Peter 3:10–11).

Let us begin with the word "elements." The English word comes from the Latin *elementum,* which, in turn, is a translation of the Greek word *stoicheion,* the word Peter uses here. Various meanings are attached to the word, including the idea of the letters of the alphabet, of a simple sound of speech, and also of the letters of the alphabet placed in order. It was used in the realm of physics to describe the components into which matter is divided. In today's English, we would use the word "atoms" to translate it. As the letters of the alphabet are the component parts of words, so atoms are the component parts of the elements and of matter.

The word for "dissolved" comes from *luo,* meaning "to break up, destroy, melt." It is sometimes translated "unloose," as when John the Baptist said he was not worthy to "unloose" the latchet of Christ's shoe (Luke 3:16). The Lord also used the word after raising Lazarus. "Loose him," He said (John 11:44). Peter, using the available words of his day, foretold a coming great conflagration of the heavens and the earth, implying that the elemental particles of matter (which we now call "atoms") will be dissolved, untied, released. Their energies, hitherto imprisoned, will be set free to cause a fearful holocaust.

The expression, "a great noise," comes from the word *rhoizedon* found only here (2 Peter 3:10). W. E. Vine says the word signifies a "'rushing sound,' as of roaring flames." The phrase "fervent heat" comes from *kausoo,* a medical word noting a fever. Peter tells us all this will take place at the very end of time.

It is comforting to know that *God* will press that button, not man. The thousand-year reign of Christ will come and go before this final conflagration described by Peter will take place. Some minor nuclear activity may take place in the tribulation period (Rev. 16:2), but the church will be gone before then; and God Himself will hold back the final nuclear woe until all His own, including His millennial hosts, are far beyond its reach.

Devotion 81

We Shall Be Like Him

1 John 3:1–2

We shall be like him," John says, "for we shall see him as he is." That points to *love* beyond all human *comprehension* and to *life* beyond all human *comparison.* John draws our attention to four features of that wondrous life.

There is, first, *an indisputable fact*: "Beloved, now are we the sons of God." There can be no room for uncertainty about that. God has said so, and God cannot lie. Now, right now, we are the children of God. "For ever, O Lord, thy word is settled in heaven" (Ps. 119:89).

There is an old story about the woman who accepted Christ through reading John 3:16. The counselor showed her where the verse was in her Bible and marked it for her. Later on that night, she had doubts. She felt the Devil was attacking her newfound faith. She was a simple soul, but wise. She decided that the darkest place in the room was under the bed, so that was where the Devil must be. She found John 3:16 in her Bible. She put her finger on the verse. She thrust the Bible under the bed. "Here," she said, "read it for yourself!" Now *are we* (right *now*) "the sons of God." We can read it for ourselves. There can be no doubt.

There is, however, *an influencing restriction* because there is something that is "not yet." John says, "It doth not yet appear what we shall be" (1 John 3:2). Our thoughts are too dull, our minds too slow, our imaginations too poor, our experience too small, and we have too little to go on for us to be able to grasp the wonders of the world to come. When Paul tried to describe what he had experienced when caught up to the third heaven, all he could say, when he came back down to earth, was "It is untranslatable!" (2 Cor. 12:4). When John tried to describe the wonders of the world to come, he resorted at once to symbolic language (Rev. 4–5). The Bible contains a strange mixture of things vividly real and hard as concrete and things mystical, ethereal, and beyond our grasp. God says, "Not yet!" when we try to probe too far.

There is also *an indescribable result.* "We shall be like Him," John says (I John 3:2). Imagine being like *Him* for all the endless ages of eternity—like Him in thought, and word, and deed; like Him in body, soul, and spirit; like Him in character, conduct, and conversation! We sing of our present earthly experience, of our longing to be like Him—

Be like Jesus, this my song,
In the home and in the throng;
Be like Jesus, all day long!
I would be like Jesus.[1]

At best we achieve only a vague resemblance to Him down here; but we know that when He shall appear, we shall be like Him.

Finally, there is *an infallible reason*: "We shall be like him; for we shall see him as he is." John had once experienced the soul-thrilling rapture of such a vision. It was on the Mount of Transfiguration (Matt. 17:1–8), though he does not speak of it in his gospel. The synoptic writers had already told that story, the story of a vision of glory, of the visitors from another world, and of a voice from heaven. John had been there along with Peter and James. He had seen the Lord's clothes ablaze with light, His face beaming like the sun. One day we are going to see Him just like that. We shall see Him as He is, in all the splendor of His humanity and in all the effulgence of His deity. Instantly, eternally, and gloriously we shall be like Him. Well has John Nelson Darby written:

And is it so—I shall be like Thy Son?
Is this the grace which He for me has won?
Father of glory! Thought beyond all thought,
In glory to His own blest likeness brought.

Yet, it must be! Thy love had not its rest
Were Thy redeemed not with Thee fully blessed,
That love that gives not as the world, but shares
All it possesses with its loved co-heirs.[2]

---

1. James Rowe, "I Would Be Like Jesus," 1911.
2. J. N. Darby, "And Is It So?" 1872.

Devotion 82

As He Is

1 John 4:17

"As he is, so are we in this world." What could be *simpler* than that? There are just nine words, all of one syllable, and six of them with only two letters—"As he is, so are we in this world." Yet, what could be *sublimer* than that? The text is so complex it is hard to know where to begin. Let us begin with Him.

We note, first, *the plan*. We are to be like Him. But that is not quite so simple as it sounds. We are reminded of the little boy who oversimplified his situation. A man asked him his name. He said, "My name is George Washington." The man said, "Well, if your name is George Washington, you'd better make sure you behave like George Washington." "Ah can't help but live like George Washington," the boy replied. "Ah is George Washington."

"As he is!" When we think of Him as He is, we realize, of course, that He is not as He was. He is living a *transformed life*. Up until about two thousand years ago, He lived an eternal life, as the uncreated, self-existing Son of the living God, invisible and infinite. Then something happened. He was born! He became a man, and in Him, now, and forever, "dwelleth all the fulness of the Godhead bodily" (Col. 2:9).

Moreover, He lives a *triumphant life*. He is God manifest in flesh. In His life down here on earth, He triumphed over sin, over Satan, and over situations. As a babe and as a boy, at home and at play, in the school and in the synagogue, as the village carpenter and as the miracle-working Christ, He lived in triumph. Not once, in thought or word or deed, did He deviate from the path of obedience to His Father in heaven. His foes tried to get rid of Him by putting Him to death, but He rose a victor from the dark domain. Now He has ascended and sits, in a human, though resurrected, body as God over all, blessed forevermore, on the throne of His Father in heaven.

Now comes *the pledge*—"As he is, so are we." We, too, have experienced a change. We, too, live a *transformed life.* We have been born again. At the time of our conversion, the Holy Spirit indwelt our body and our being. We are now inhabited by God, for our human spirit has been quickened by God's Holy Spirit. As He became flesh and dwelt among us, as God manifest in flesh, so now we have become people indwelt by God.

This means that we now are to live a *triumphant life,* victorious over sin, Satan, and situations. Our life is a continuation of His life, made possible by the indwelling, filling, and anointing of the Holy Spirit. The use of the formula "as . . . even so" in the Bible always depicts an exact similarity.

Finally, mention is made of *the place.* All are ready to agree that we are to be like Him in heaven. John himself says as much: "We shall be like him; for we shall see him as he is." (I John 3:2). But note this: "As he is, so are we *in this world*" (4:17). It is not only then and there, but also here and now.

A Christian lady saw a shoeless boy gazing longingly at shoes in a shop window. Touched, she took him in and bought him some shoes and socks, washed his feet, and put them on him. "Please, ma'am," said the little boy, "are you Christ's wife?"

As He is, so are we in this world.

Devotion 83

The Way of Cain

Jude 11

Cain went out from the presence of God a marked man, a rebel, unbowed and unrepentant. So, God had rejected his altar and his religion! Well, he would live without God. For a while he was "a fugitive and a vagabond . . . in the earth" (Gen. 4:12), but in time he decided to make his own way in the world. And so he did. He founded a great but godless civilization, one that was bent his way. The Holy Spirit calls it "the way of Cain." Cain organized human life and society into a way of living that left God out. The Spirit of God records a number of things about the godless way of Cain.

It was *materialistic.* Job calls it "the old way." He tells how people told God to leave them alone while at the same time demanding that He prove Himself to them by showing what He could do for them. Their houses were filled with good things, and they congratulated themselves on their successes and ignored the fact that even their material prosperity really came from God (Job 22:15–18).

It was *humanistic.* If Cain could not have his own religion, he would have no religion at all. He would become captain of his own soul and master of his own destiny. Of the twelve people mentioned by name in the line of Cain and his descendants, only two retained any semblance of the knowledge of God—Mehujael and Methusael (Gen. 4:16–24).

It was *prolific.* There was a population explosion. "Men began to multiply" (Gen. 6:1). This ever-increasing world population created an ever-expanding market for goods and services, especially as the antediluvian society became increasingly sophisticated.

It was *urbanistic.* The growing population abandoned the countryside for the city. The population became increasingly urban. God put people in a garden; Cain put them in a city, and the city became an artificial paradise catering to the wants and needs of mankind.

It was *hedonistic*; that is to say, it was a pleasure-driven society. The entertainment business was born, introduced by Jubal, who invented music and gave people a beat to enliven their days.

It was *pragmatic*. Tubal-cain brought the world through an industrial revolution and gave it a growing industry based on science, engineering, and technology.

It was *agnostic*. An agnostic is a person who says you can't know—specifically, that you can't know God. This was a marked feature of Cainite civilization. It was godless. The Cainites ignored the testimony of Enoch (Jude 14) and the preaching of Noah. Their minds were blinded by the god of this world. They "knew not" was the Lord's final verdict on them all. (Matt. 24:39).

It was *demonic*. The human soul abhors a vacuum, so those who ignore God often fall prey to evil and deceiving spirits. So it was with the Cainites who delved into the deep things of Satan and produced a "New Age" movement that, in turn, introduced strange and deadly occult phenomena. A hybrid race appeared, mirrored in later times by the fallen gods of Olympus of Greek mythology (Gen. 6:4).

It was *pornographic*. "Every imagination of the thoughts of [people's] heart[s] was only evil continually," the Holy Spirit says (Gen. 6:5). Along with that, there was a breakdown of the primeval law of marriage. Moreover, women became prominent in Cainite society, and polygamy was accepted as a lifestyle.

It was *anarchistic*. Society failed to exert restraint upon crime. Consequently, "the earth was filled with violence" (Gen. 6:11). The popular lifestyle was openly permissive, and everyone "did his own thing" with the nod and approval of society.

It was *antagonistic*. The seventh from Adam in Cain's line was Lamech, an openly polygamous man and a boastful murderer (Gen. 4:19, 23–24). This wicked man even shook his fist in the face of God and told Him to stay out of his affairs.

It was *fatalistic*. The idea that God might have some say about all this was ignored. Cainite society ran right through the center of a fault line where God stored up His wrath. The building of Noah's ark struck the Cainites as ludicrous. What was going to happen would happen, and there was nothing anyone could do about it. As for building an ark, that was a typical crackpot idea of the Sethites. An ark indeed!

Such was the way of Cain. In the end God destroyed that wicked society and its people. The flood came and took them all away, as God said it would.

Devotion 84

What a Way to Begin

Revelation 1:4–5

The book of Revelation begins with a burst of names that set forth the glory of the Lord Jesus. He is called "him which is, and which was, and which is to come." He is called "Jesus Christ, who is the faithful witness, and the first begotten of the dead, and the prince of the kings of the earth." Names! This book is "the revelation," the unveiling, of Jesus Christ. Throughout the Old Testament period, God's principle way of revealing Himself was by means of His names. There are three primary names for God: Elohim (El, Elah), Jehovah, and Adonai (Adon). There are three compound names linked with El: El Shaddai (Almighty God), El Elyon (God Most High), and El Olam (Everlasting God). And there are various compound names linked with Jehovah: Jehovah Elohim (Lord God), Adonai Jehovah (Lord God), Jehovah Sabaoth (Lord of Hosts), and so on. These names tell us much about God. Here, in the opening chapter of the Apocalypse, we catch five glimpses of our Lord in glory, fresh revelations of Him, by means of His names.

He is *the infinite one,* "him which is, and which was, and which is to come." He is the one who transcends time. Past, present, and future are all gathered up and put beneath His feet. What we actually have here is a paraphrase of the Old Testament name Jehovah. The name implies that God always was, always is, and always will be.

He is *the incarnate one,* "Jesus Christ." That is the name He assumed when He came down here to live. "Jesus" reveals Him as the Man; "Christ" reveals Him as the Messiah. That was how John knew Him best—very much a man—yet, he also knew Him as God. He is the one of whom we sing:

> Fairest of all the earth beside,
> Chiefest of all unto Thy bride,

Fullness divine in Thee I see,
Beautiful Man of Calvary![1]

He is that longed-for "daysman" for whom Job sought (Job 9:33), that one Mediator between God and man.

He is the *inerrant one,* "the faithful witness" (Rev. 1:5). He is the one who spoke for God with unfailing compassion, unerring comprehension, and unflinching courage. He spoke with authority and not as the Scribes. He witnessed to the truth without fear or favor. He spoke in a particularly pungent way, conveying truth in a memorable, undiluted form. And He was never wrong. He never had to retract a single statement and never had to apologize for anything He said. People's hearts were an open book to Him. Even His enemies said: "Never man spake like this man" (John 7:46).

He is *the initial one,* "the first begotten of the dead" (Rev. 1:5). As J. B. Phillips puts it: "Life from nothing began through Him; life from the dead began through Him" (Col. 1:16).

Death could not hold its prey, . . .
He tore the bars away . . .
Up from the grave He arose,
With a mighty triumph o'er His foes.[2]

All others die, victims to the dread reaper's scythe. Even the half dozen raised by Elijah, Elisha, and Jesus died again. Jesus was the "first begotten of the dead," the Pioneer of a new race of resurrected and raptured saints.

He is *the invincible one,* "prince of the kings of the earth" (Rev. 1:5). All earthly crowns will be cast at His feet when He comes back to reign. His coming empire here on earth will last for a thousand years, and it will stretch from the river to the ends of the earth (Zech. 9:10). Indeed,

Jesus shall reign where'er the sun
Doth his successive journeys run;

1. Manis P. Ferguson, "That Man of Calvary."
2. Robert Lowry, "Christ Arose," 1874.

His kingdom spread from shore to shore,
Till moons shall wax and wane no more.[3]

The rest of the book of Revelation is the outworking in history of these things.

---

3. Isaac Watts, "Jesus Shall Reign," 1719.

Devotion 85

Grace Be unto You, and Peace
Part 1

Revelation 1:4–6

Grace be unto you, and peace." Thus the book of Revelation begins—more like a Pauline epistle than a great apocalypse. Here is a book that deals primarily with judgment, but God begins it with grace. In this book we see people getting what they deserve—judgment after judgment from a God whose patience is exhausted at last. The floodtides of His wrath, which have been dammed back since Calvary, are now released. The dams burst. The pent-up oceans of His holy anger against sin and against the murder of His Son pour out now in all their fury. But first, God speaks of His grace. God tells people that judgment is His strange work. He would far rather offer them His grace. Grace, as the word is used in Scripture, is the outpouring of God's unmerited kindness to sinners.

Years ago a reclaimed drunkard named Sam Duncannon used to haunt the halls of the Glasgow mission in Scotland. He was poor. He was simple, but he was saved. He collected pictures, and he collected poems. He would find a picture and paste it onto some cardboard; then he would find a matching poem and paste that alongside the picture. Then he would give these picture poems to the derelicts who came through the mission, hoping they might bring some brightness into their lives.

One day someone gave Sam Duncannon a picture of Niagara Falls. He loved it. He looked and looked for a poem to put beside it. But he could not find one.

Then one day D. L. Moody came to the Glasgow mission, along with Ira Sankey. Mr. Sankey got up to sing, and at once Sam knew he had found the words he wanted for his picture of Niagara Falls. This is what Mr. Sankey sang:

Have you on the Lord believed?
Still there's more to follow.
Of His grace have you received?
Still there's more to follow.
Oh the grace the Father shows!
Still there's more to follow.
Freely He His grace bestows,
Still there's more to follow.

More and more, more and more,
Always more to follow,
Oh, His matchless, boundless love!
Still there's more to follow.[1]

Such indeed is the boundless grace of God. "Grace be unto you!" Grace to defy the Devil to the very end! Grace to win souls from beneath the very throne of the Beast! Grace poured out upon the two witnesses and then superabundantly upon the 144,000 witnesses until the converts of the judgment age to come promise to outnumber all those of history.

And yet more grace! Grace to send an angel with "the everlasting gospel" to win still more souls before the bowls of wrath are outpoured (Rev. 14:6–7). Indeed, so great is God's desire for lost people to be saved, right down to the last possible moment, that He reduces the angel's message here to the lowest possible terms. Here is no elaborate New Testament theology. Here is no demand for good works of any kind. It is the primeval gospel, the simplest, most universal beliefs available to all people everywhere based on the evidence of creation and conscience (the kind of thing we have in Rom. 1:18–20). "Fear God, and give glory to him; for the hour of his judgment is come: and worship him that made heaven, and earth, and the sea, and the fountains of waters" (Rev. 14:7). There will be no time left to discuss the profound theology of the cross—besides the prerogative of preaching Christ and Him crucified is not given to angels but to humans. But we alas have failed. With judgment fires already poised on high and about to descend, there are still untold millions still untold, so an angel is sent. He calls for the barest essentials of belief God can accept; and one last, burning call is given from heaven. Such is our God—a God of matchless grace.

---

1. Philip P. Bliss, "Have You on the Lord Believed?" 1873.

Devotion 86

Grace Be unto You, and Peace
Part 2

Revelation 1:4–6

Grace be unto you, and peace!" Imagine that! What a way to begin the Apocalypse, especially when the book of Revelation deals with the very opposite of peace. Its themes are those of bloodshed and war. It rings with the din and noise of strife. It tells of carnage and conflict; of earthquakes, pestilence, famine and woe; of purges and persecutions that dwarf all those of history. It tells of the crash of mighty empires, of anarchy, oppression, terror, and wrath. It tells of an incarnate Beast, indwelt and driven by the Devil. It tells of war in heaven and war on earth. It goes from one horror to another. Its martyrs are countless. Blood flows in crimson tides. Thunders roll, stars fall from heaven, seas turn to blood, seals are broken, trumpets are blown, and vials of wrath are poured out. Plagues surge up from the bottomless pit in the form of vast, countless armies mobilized by Satan himself. Soldiers by the millions march to Megiddo. Then the heavens split asunder, and there is a final invasion from outer space. It is Jesus, coming again, backed by the armies of heaven!

But first, God speaks one word—"Peace!" God would much rather make peace than wage war, but this is God's final peace offer. When He came the first time, the heralds from on high offered peace. When He appeared in the upper room, in resurrection power, He proclaimed peace. Now, before the end-time wars and woes, He extends an olive branch one more time—"Peace!" He says. "Peace."

I was just a boy when World War II broke out in Britain. It broke out on a Sunday morning. In one of our churches, a man came in late. He had just heard the news. We were at war. He gave the news, and a solemn hush came over the people. War! A man got up and gave out a hymn. It went like this:

Peace, perfect peace, in this dark world of sin?
The blood of Jesus whispers peace within.

Peace, perfect peace, with sorrows surging 'round?
On Jesus' bosom naught but calm is found.

Peace, perfect peace, with loved ones far away?
In Jesus' keeping we are safe, and they.

Peace, perfect peace, our future all unknown?
Jesus we know, and He is on the throne.

Peace, perfect peace, death shadowing us and ours?
Jesus has vanquished death and all its powers.

It is enough: earth's struggles soon shall cease
And Jesus call to Heaven's perfect peace.[1]

It is with some such thought in mind that Jesus begins this Apocalypse with an offer of lasting peace.

"Grace be unto you, and peace." Yes, indeed, for grace and peace break through at last. The storm clouds roll away. The drums of war are stilled, the earth itself is purged with fire, and there emerges a new heaven and a new earth where all is grace and peace.

---

1. Edward H. Bickersteth, "Peace, Perfect Peace," 1875.

Devotion 87

I Fell at His Feet as Dead

The Unknowable One

Revelation 1:13–17

John had known Him long years ago, before ever His name became a household word. He had often seen Him in His peasant, homespun, seamless robe. He had seen Him at work in the carpenter's shop, every saw cut, joint, and decoration a masterpiece. He had caught a glimpse of the glory that was His on the holy mount. But there had never been anything like this, the vision glorious on the Patmos Isle. He fell at His feet as dead. He tries to tell us what he saw, tries to translate into human speech the marvels and mysteries of heaven. The best he can do is to fall back on symbols. There were ten separate details that were impressed upon his soul.

First, John saw the Lord as the *unknowable* One. So much about Him was concealed. "He was clothed," John says, "with a garment down to the foot."

John remembered the robe that Jesus wore the day that He was crucified. That robe had been flung over His shoulders and back, wet with His blood from the thongs of the scourge. The soldiers rolled their dice to see who would have it as his prize.

Our attention is drawn to *the garment,* the seamless robe Jesus wore when He was crucified. There were five articles of dress—the headpiece, the sandals, the outer covering, the girdle, and the seamless robe, which was of more value than all the rest. There were four soldiers assigned to each cross. They had stood stolidly by as Christ was scourged. They had laughed with derision as Christ was mocked, in an imitation robe and wearing a crown of thorns.

But now the horseplay was over. The mocking purple was snatched away and His own clothes tossed to Him. He put on the robe. Blood from the scourging stained it. Perhaps John could remember the first time Jesus put it on, a present from His mother, perhaps, or an aunt, or a friend. John would certainly remember this last time He put it on, over His tortured body, in Pilate's judgment hall.

Our attention is drawn to *the gamblers.* The four soldiers assigned to Christ's cross made short work of the shoes, the girdle, the headgear, and the outer covering. But what about the robe? It was too valuable to be torn into pieces and divided up. So they found their dice and gambled for it. So careless, so callous is this world toward the Son of God.

But then after all, there was *the goal.* For this very act of gambling was of God. It is the subject of prophecy (Ps. 22:18) and of history (Matt. 27:35). Doubtless the winning soldier cleansed the robe, and stuffed it into his bag. Then he marched off with it into oblivion. And it is a good thing he did, or an apostate church in a later age would have made a relic of it, put it in a shrine, and fabricated legends of its imagined healing power. It would be venerated and worshiped, thus displacing God's Son.

Some 730 years before, Isaiah described another robe, one not worn, as yet, on earth. He tells us that the Messiah will come striding up from Edom, His garment red with blood from treading out the vintage where the grapes of wrath were stored (Isa. 63:1–3).

But John saw beyond all this. In the first of ten awesome sights, he saw the Savior once again arrayed in a robe. All he saw was His head, His hands, and His feet. The robe concealed the rest. That all-concealing robe reminds us of how little we know of Him.

What did He do between His birth and His baptism? We do not know. What did He do day by day, hour by hour, in the years of His ministry? We do not know. The Gospels themselves are mere fragments, hardly more than memos. John's, for instance, devotes half of its length to the events of one week. Only thirty-six miracles are recorded in the Gospels. He performed thousands.

The seamless robe He wore here spoke symbolically of humanity. There is something very human about a man wearing a robe. The robe John saw concealed most of the all-mysterious person of the now ascended Son of the living God. There is so much more about Him yet to be revealed. The book of Revelation is the "Apocalypse," the "unveiling" of Jesus Christ. But when we reach the end of it and John puts down his pen, we still feel that there remains much more to be said. Our few short years of time enable us to merely touch the hem of that garment down to the foot. It will take us all eternity to know Him as we ought.

Devotion 88

I Fell at His Feet as Dead

The Unemotional One

Revelation 1:13–17

John was down there in the dust of the marble quarry, flat on his face, as one already dead. He raised his eyes a little and saw the hem of a garment. He raised his head. All he could see was that robe. Almost all else was concealed. The One at whose feet he lay was the *unknowable* One. Very little could be seen of Him; still less could be known.

As he gazed higher, he saw that this one was girded across the breast "with a golden girdle." He was the *unemotional* One. The breast is the seat of the emotions, as the head is the seat of the intellect. The girdle symbolizes restraint. The girdle was worn in John's day to hold back a person's flowing robes, to restrain them lest they should get in the way. The girdle John saw was a golden girdle. Gold is a biblical symbol for God. In the tabernacle, for instance, the boards were made of acacia wood, the common, gnarled, and twisted wood of the desert; but they were overlaid with gold. The wood spoke of the Lord's down-to-earth humanity; the gold spoke of His deity. The golden girdle John saw wound around the heart of Jesus draws our attention to the fact that His emotions are now not only restrained but they also are divinely restrained, held back by God.

It is not, of course, as though the Lord Jesus *cannot* feel. Of course He can! He is our Great High Priest, even at this moment, "touched with the feeling of our infirmities" (Heb. 4:15). He has been described as "a man of sorrows, and acquainted with grief" (Isa. 53:3). He taught His disciples that they should rejoice with those who rejoice and weep with those who weep. Nobody knew this better than John. It is no accident that the first miracle of Christ's ministry, recorded in John's gospel, was performed at a wedding, and the last one was performed at a funeral—life's gladdest and life's saddest hours. The Lord Jesus is deeply moved in His heart by the terrible things sin has done in this world. Three times we read that He wept. He wept at the tomb of Lazarus for an individual. He wept on the Mount of Olives, for a Christ-rejecting nation. He wept and wept in dark Gethsemane for all the children of Adam's ruined race.

And there was joy too, "joy unspeakable and full of glory" (I Peter 1:8). It was for the joy set before Him that He endured the cross. He stood with the cheering section of glory to add His joyful welcome when Stephen, battered but triumphant, burst into glory.

But now all that is put under divine restraint. All emotion is held in check. He is about to begin His "strange work" and launch an offensive of judgment and wrath upon this world. No wonder all feelings are now firmly held back. Emotion must not be allowed to feed His fury or to cause pity to mitigate His wrath. Let all people be advised that the mercy seat has now become the judgment seat. The hour of His wrath has come. There are no scenes in the Bible more sobering or more solemn than this, or more terrible than those about to be unveiled.

Devotion 89

I Fell at His Feet as Dead

The Unimpeachable One

Revelation 1:14

John was still at Jesus' feet as one dead. In past days, he often had leaned on the Lord's breast, but not now. Not even the blinding vision on the holy mount, when Moses and Elijah appeared and Jesus was transfigured, remotely resembled this. The One in whose dread presence he now lay prostrate on the ground was the *unknowable* One. He was the *unemotional* One, girt around the breast with a golden girdle. John ventures another look. He sees that Christ's head and hair are white like wool, like snow. He is also the *unimpeachable* One, the Holy One, holy beyond all thought.

It was not this way that John remembered Him, with hair whiter than the driven snow. Nor was it this way that the Shulamite described her beloved—her beloved who so majestically pictures our Beloved.

Solomon, we remember, had abducted the Shulamite and had sought to overwhelm her with his wealth and words. Unable to achieve his ends, he turned her over to the court women, hoping that these harem beauties might persuade her to yield her affections to him. No way! Her heart and her affections were already engaged to another, to her beloved shepherd. The exasperated court women burst out, "What is thy beloved more than another beloved?" (Song 5:9). What does he have that Solomon, prince of this world, does not have? The Shulamite described Him: "My beloved is white and ruddy," she said. He is "the chiefest among ten thousand. His head is as the most fine gold, his locks are bushy, and black as a raven" (vv. 10–11). Thus she described her beloved—and our Beloved, as seen through Old Testament eyes.

What happened to turn those locks of His from the blackness of a raven's wing to the whiteness of the virgin snow?

In the IMAX version of Niagara Falls, we see the first person ever to go over the falls in a barrel. This woman was one of the few to survive. She took a small, black kitten with her in the barrel to be her companion on the nightmare ride. When they emerged, the kitten had turned white. It was the moviemaker's way of reminding us that a horrific experience can turn black hair white.

"His locks," said the Shulamite, "are bushy, and black as a raven." "His head and his hairs were white like wool, as white as snow," says John (Rev. 1:14). Something of a horrifying nature must have happened. And so it did—*Calvary.*

That ordeal had ever been before Him, from before the foundation of the world. It assumed more concrete form when, as a boy of twelve, on the occasion of the Passover in Jerusalem, He contemplated the death of the Lamb. It took a new nightmare turn in Gethsemane when, as the poet puts it,

> For me it was in the garden
> He prayed, "Not My will but Thine."
> He shed no tears for His own griefs,
> But sweat drops of blood for mine.[1]

And then it burst upon Him in all its horror at the place called Calvary, when He who knew no sin was made sin for us and when He, the source of all life, tasted death for everyone.

Since then, His hair has been white. Whenever we look at Him, through all the endless ages yet to be, that snowy hair will remind us of how greatly He must have loved us to suffer so.

---

1. Charles H. Gabriel, "I Stand Amazed in the Presence," 1905.

Devotion 90

I Fell at His Feet as Dead

The Undeceivable One

REVELATION 1:14

Perhaps it was His eyes that struck the prone apostle with the greatest terror, for he said, "his eyes were as a flame of fire." He saw Christ now as the *undeceivable* One, able to penetrate through all subterfuge as white-hot concentrated heat can slice through steel. Fire can consume suns and stars and mighty galaxies. Nothing can hide from fire. When He lived on earth Jesus wept with those who wept. His eyes were a fountain of tears. No more. They are now a flame of fire.

Charles Dickens tells us what happened to the violent robber, Bill Sikes, after he had murdered Nancy, the woman who loved him. "At length the sun shed its light into the room where the murderer cowered still, afraid to take his eyes off the corpse." Once he threw a rug over it, but then he imagined those staring eyes moving toward him, so he tore the rug away. With the first light of day, the criminal fled, but the eyes followed him. Indeed, it seemed to him that the corpse itself followed him, but especially "the eyes."

In the end the murderer, Bill Sikes, was cornered in the attic of a house with a howling mob outside and no place to go. Only one hope remained. He opened the window and crawled out onto the roof. The crowd saw him and let out a roar. The criminal tied a rope around a chimney, made a loop in it, and passed it over his head. He intended to place it under his arms and lower himself down to the river. But then he saw the eyes. With a yell of terror, he lost his balance. The rope around his neck ran swiftly through its coils, and he was jerked violently to his death. He swung lifeless between heaven and earth, killed by those staring eyes.[1]

---

1. Charles Dickens, *Oliver Twist,* 1838.

But those were only the eyes of a murdered girl. Who can imagine the dread terror that will be inspired in all, at last, by the eyes of a murdered Christ now resurrected? Those eyes are as a flame of fire, and they see everything and miss nothing.

I remember the text that hung upon my boyhood bedroom wall: "Thou God seest me," it said. The words were first spoken by poor, ill-treated, runaway Hagar when God came to her as once He had come to Abraham (Gen. 16:13). It was a comforting thought to her, that God saw her. It was intended to be a comforting thought to me. But it had another and a different message—"Thou God seest me." It brought to memory my boyish sins, sins that God saw. It ceased to be a comforting text; it became a condemning text.

"Thou God seest me!" It will be the tormented cry of the lost at the great white throne, as they realize they have no secrets and no hiding place. In vain do they call on the mountains and hills to fall on them and blot out the terror of those all-seeing eyes. And those eyes of His will follow them out into a lost eternity, haunting them forever and ever. But as for us who have come to love the Lord, the words, "Thou God seest me," are transformed by the chemistry of Calvary. They threaten us no more. They thrill us now. He sees!

Devotion 91

I Fell at His Feet as Dead

The Undeterrable One

REVELATION 1:15

John looked away from those fiery eyes, and his gaze dropped to the Master's feet. "His feet," he says, "[were] like unto fine brass, as if they burned in a furnace." Brass is a common symbol in Scripture for judgment. Nothing can halt the march of those feet when once He rises up to judge the world. He is the *undeterrable* One. John saw those feet when they were nailed to a cross. He saw them in the upper room on the day Christ rose. He saw them step from the brow of Olivet into the sky. But we must pause and trace their ordained path.

Those feet broke through the silence of a past eternity and awoke the echoes of the everlasting hills. A thousand billion galaxies were but cobblestones beneath them, mere pebbles on His pathway across the vastness of the universe.

But listen now! Those feet step out of eternity into time; and they have become baby feet, for the path He chose led through the confines of a virgin's womb to a human body just like ours. Baby feet they were, challenging a mother's busy fingers to knit little booties and things to keep them warm.

And now they have become the busy feet of a boy, running here and there, climbing trees, splashing in a water hole, walking back and forth to school, hopping along to the synagogue, and on into the carpenter's shop.

What blessed feet they were! They took Him through Samaria when anyone else would have gone miles out of the way, around and across Jordan in order not to go through Samaria. But He knew of a well there at Sychar and of a woman, shopworn and weary, a woman He wanted to meet and bless and transform. Then on to other people in other places those feet took Him—to Nicodemus in Jerusalem, to Jairus in Galilee, to Zacchaeus near Jericho. Those blessed feet of His were ever on the go until He had visited each corner of the Promised Land, taking Him by way of Calvary to the haunted halls of hades, and then on back to earth, to heaven, and to home.

But hark! All is now changed. Those feet are now like burnished brass. Their tramp shakes the earth to its foundation, in ways the Psalms describe (Pss. 18; 29).

Down here on earth the tramp of other feet are heard. The teeming millions of the East break away from the empire of the Beast. They mobilize soldiers by the millions and march them to Megiddo. The West is mobilized in response. The tramp of Western armies is heard across many an ancient battlefield. They, too, are marching to Megiddo.

The issue in this "war to end all war" is simple enough. Who will rule the world—East or West? So the stage is set for conflict and carnage such as the world has never known in all its long and war-filled past.

But suddenly, above all the noise and din on earth, there comes a terrifying sound—marching feet on high, feet of burning brass, feet shod now to trample out the vintage of the earth. The heavens rend asunder with a roar. Satan's hosts on high are swept aside, of no account. The Lord is passing through the heavens on His way to earth. The hour of His wrath has come. God-hating people, Christ-rejecting people, gathered in the cockpit of the world, are face to face with doom. Those trampling feet make short work of the millions at Megiddo and move on their relentless way to touch down on Olivet. It splits asunder with a roar. The Lord has come at last! None can bar His way. Heaven is His throne, and earth His footstool—and every knee shall bow to own Him as Lord.

The whole creation groans, anticipating the coming of its absent Lord, straining toward that day, looking forward to the day when He at last will tread the earth once more.

Devotion 92

I Fell at His Feet as Dead

The Unanswerable One

Revelation 1:15

There John lay, still lying at those feet, as one dead. Only now sight gives way to sound. He hears a voice. Oh, how often he had heard that voice in those far-off Galilean days, the voice of Jesus. Sometimes it was sweeter than the honeycomb, saying to the sinful woman, "Neither do I condemn thee: go, and sin no more" (John 8:11); sometimes it was softer than the whisper of the wind in the willows, saying to the dying thief, "Today shalt thou be with me in paradise" (Luke 23:43); and sometimes it was sterner than cold steel, saying to His disciples, "One of you is a devil" (John 6:70). How John remembered that voice! Even His enemies felt its force. The Sermon on the Mount, the mystery parables, the discourse on the Mount of Olives—truly, "never man spake like this man" (John 7:46).

But now all is changed. "His voice," John says, is "as the sound of many waters" (Rev. 1:15). He is the *unanswerable* One. On the Canadian side of Niagara Falls, the visitor can go down an elevator shaft to a long corridor, which brings one to a platform underneath the falls. Some fourteen million people a year come to see these awesome falls. Every minute 34.5 million gallons of water go over the edge into the boiling cauldron below. It is a place of roaring cataracts, swirling whirlpools, and towering, rocky banks. And oh how that sound of many waters drowns out all other sounds. The Native Americans called it "the place of thundering waters." Such is now the voice of Jesus preparing for judgment. There will be no discussion, no debate next time He speaks.

One of the mysteries of this present age is *His silence*. It is a silence absolute and prolonged—for nearly two thousand years. But it is not the silence of indifference. It is the silence of a great sabbatical rest. The Son of God died at the hands of sinful humans. God might well have reacted in wrath, with a roar like thunder, with a shout, with the voice of the archangel, and with the trump of doom. Instead, there was a silence, a silence that says that the way is open still for even the guiltiest to draw near and be forgiven.

Little do people realize what they are asking for when they challenge God to break that silence. He will break it one of these days, and when He does it will mean the withdrawal of the amnesty, the end of the day of grace, and the dawn of the day of wrath.

So John lay there, as that dread voice, like the thundering waters of Niagara, drowned out all other sounds. The voice of the returning Christ will silence all human words and will confuse even the thoughts of the mind. It will be the prelude to wrath. The silence will be broken at long last, and woe will betide the world! Every mouth will be stopped. The whole world, guilty before God, will be judged. With fury unimagined, the apocalypse will come. Then, when even all *that* noise is stilled, lost people will find themselves standing exposed, ashamed, and silenced as the words of accusation and doom thunder and roar in their ears. John could find no other words to describe what will happen when God speaks again—"His voice [is] as the sound of many waters," he says. And he leaves it at that.

Devotion 93

I Fell at His Feet as Dead

The Unparalleled One

Revelation 1:16

Still on his face, John ventured a further look at the awesome One who stood beside him. "And he had in his right hand seven stars," John said. He was the *unparalleled* One, the One who rules the stars. Who but God alone could do such a thing? Take our own sun, for instance. It is a moderate star, numbered neither among the stellar giants nor the stellar dwarfs. It weighs 2.2 billion, billion, billion tons. It contains 99.86 percent of the mass of our solar system. Solar scientists affirm that the sun has a lifespan of about ten billion years. One second of the sun's energy is equal to thirteen million times the annual mean electricity consumption of the United States. John saw the Lord holding seven such stars in His right hand. That, of course, amounts to nothing to One who includes omnipotence among His attributes. Let us beware of a concept of our Lord that is too small.

It is evident, of course, that whatever lessons we can draw from this picture of the might and magnificence of our Lord, the Holy Spirit does not intend us to take the stars literally. It is clearly symbolic. Indeed, we are not left to speculate about this because the Spirit Himself interprets the symbolism. The lampstands John saw represented seven churches, churches that existed in John's day, churches he knew well and he had often visited in days gone by. The stars symbolized the angels of those churches (Rev. 1:20).

There are various ranks and responsibilities among the angels. Satan's fallen angels include principalities and powers, the rulers of this world's darkness, and wicked spirits in high places. God's angels include thrones and dominions, high dignitaries of heaven. There are countless legions of messenger angels, such as Gabriel; martial angels, led by Michael; and ministering angels, who attend to the needs of God's people in enemy territory on earth.

Children have their guardian angels, who report all child abuse directly to God. *Christians* have their angels—both Peter and Paul saw theirs. *Christ* had His ministering angels, and we see them caring for Him at the close of His temptation in the wilderness and after His agony in Gethsemane. Now we learn that *churches* have their guardian angels. There is a passing confirmation of this in I Corinthians 11, where Paul tells ministering women to cover their heads "because of the angels" (v. 10).

Each of the seven churches of Asia had its angel. Each one reported directly to Christ, the Head of the church. He controlled their activities and held them in His right hand, the hand of power. Churches need the help of these angels, for ours is a spiritual warfare. Our ministering angels draw the line beyond which Satan and his evil spirits cannot go. Herod, for instance, was smitten when he went too far. We should be thankful for these powerful allies in our continuing battle against the forces of sin.

Devotion 94

I Fell at His Feet as Dead

The Unconquerable One

Revelation 1:16

Still in his prone position, John ventured to lift his eyes higher. "Out of his mouth," he said, "went a sharp, twoedged sword." He was the *unconquerable* One.

The sword is first seen, of all places, in connection with the garden of Eden. The fall had taken place, and the world had suddenly become a wild and wicked place. The sentence of death had been pronounced upon Adam and his posterity, though there would be a stay of execution for some for many years. Thorns and thistles were already staking their claim to the earth, and the lion's roar and the wolf's snarl were suddenly full of menace.

The guilty pair, banished from Eden, thought nostalgically of their former, safe, beautiful home. Perhaps they could go back and gain access to the Tree of Life and circumvent the sentence of death. There, ahead of them, was the garden gate. They made their way toward it. Then they saw one of the cherubim, an angelic being, with a drawn sword in its hand, barring their way. Distant death suddenly became threatening, present death. God was not going to allow them to eat of the Tree of Life, for then they would have lived forever in their sins, deathless as the angels and sinful as the hosts of hell. They turned away, haunted by the memory of that flaming sword.

The next time we see this sword, it is through the eyes of one of the last of the Old Testament prophets, Zechariah by name. "Awake, O sword, against my shepherd," he said. "Smite the shepherd, and the sheep shall be scattered" (Zech. 13:7). Centuries later his words were fulfilled. At Calvary the sword of the living God awakened, and its blade burned and blazed in the hand of God. It was plunged into the heart of Jesus. The downward thrust of that terrible, swift sword was not arrested. It was driven deep into the Savior's soul. When it was withdrawn, the blood of Jesus, gushing forward, became a crimson tide, a fountain for uncleanness opened up for all.

But we are not yet done with that sword. John on Patmos, prostrate on the ground, saw it coming out of the mouth of the Son of God. The language, of course, is symbolic. Paul says that "the sword of the Spirit" is "the word of God" (Eph. 6:17). God is now about to wreak vengeance on this world and on the wicked race that murdered His Son.

The scene changes. We are at Megiddo. The armies of the world, East and West, face each other, armed with weapons of mass destruction. With a roar, the heavens split wide, and the Son of God appears. That symbolic sword comes out of His mouth; He speaks (Rev. 19:15). One word from Him, and all is over! He speaks, and down they go! That sharp, two-edged sword has done its work. Now there will be peace upon this planet for a thousand years. The sword can rest at last.

Devotion 95

I Fell at His Feet as Dead

The Unapproachable One

Revelation 1:16

John raised his head one more time, this time to glance at the face of Jesus. He turned away blinded, dazzled. "His countenance," he said, "was as the sun shining in his strength." He was the *unapproachable* One.

John well remembered the face of Jesus, the Jesus he had known, probably since boyhood days, the Jesus whose disciple he had become. In those days, He had been the most approachable of men. Little children sensed it and climbed up on His knee. Anyone could come. Aristocratic Nicodemus could come, the woman at the well could come, and Simon the leper could come. Poor, blind Bartimaeus could come. Rich, poor, beggar, and thief all could come. And Jesus' beaming face made them welcome and put them all at ease.

But that was then. And this was now. John was looking at this same Jesus whom he and others had seen ascend bodily into heaven. But how different He looked now! Now He was as unapproachable as the sun. We cannot even look directly into the face of the sun, shining in its strength. We certainly cannot approach it. John, who had been the disciple closest to Jesus, the dearest friend of this one whose face now resembled the sun, was at His feet as dead.

Think for a moment of the sun, shining in its strength. It has a diameter of 864,000 miles. The core of the sun is subject to inconceivable pressure—a million, million pounds per square inch. The only thing that keeps the sun's core from collapsing and solidifying is its energy—energy almost beyond belief, energy sufficient to raise the internal temperature to more than 25 million degrees Fahrenheit by means of nuclear fusion. The energy resulting from this process eventually reaches the surface of the sun. It then radiates into space. The sun, we are told, shines with a constant power of 380 million billion billion watts. It takes sunlight eight minutes to travel from the sun to the earth. Solar flares, brilliant flashes of light on the sun's surface, sometimes produce energies equal to a billion hydrogen bombs. Such is the sun.

One glimpse of the face of Jesus, and all John could think of was the sun. Such will the face of Jesus be toward His foes, when He comes again. People will scream in terror at the sight. And well they might.

But for us, it will be a smiling face, aglow with all the light of heaven, with radiant love for His own.

Devotion 96

I Fell at His Feet as Dead

The Unchangeable One

Revelation 1:17

Thus John saw Jesus as the apostle lay face down in the dust, overwhelmed at the heavenly vision. He was terrified. And it is no wonder. Let us put it all together in Revelation 1. The One in whose dread presence John was filled him with fear.

1. He was the *unknowable* One, "clothed with a garment down to the foot."
2. He was the *unemotional* One, girded across the breast "with a golden girdle."
3. He was the *unimpeachable* One. "His head and his hairs were white like wool, as white as snow."
4. He was the *undeceivable* One. "His eyes were as a flame of fire."
5. He was the *undeterrable* One. "His feet [were] like unto fine brass, as if they burned in a furnace."
6. He was the *unanswerable* One. "His voice [was] as the sound of many waters."
7. He was the *unparalleled* One. "He had in his right hand seven stars."
8. He was the *unconquerable* One. "Out of his mouth went a sharp, twoedged sword."
9. He was the *unapproachable* One. "His countenance was as the sun shineth in his strength."

But there was one thing more.

10. He was the *unchangeable* One. John said, "He laid his right hand upon me, saying unto me, Fear not; I am the first and the last: I am he that liveth, and was dead; and, behold, I am alive for evermore . . . and have the keys of hell and of death."

The terrifying appearance is for His foes, not His friends. That gentle touch and that gracious voice, however, was the same. There was nothing to fear—not even death itself, for He now holds the keys of death and hell. Paul calls death the last enemy. Spurgeon says, "If death is the last enemy, then leave him till last." Jesus says, "Leave him to Me!"

John never feared again. See him there in glory, amidst scenes of grandeur. All about him are the crowned royalties of heaven. There he is, one lone man. Tears? Yes! Sorrow that not one man is fit to govern the globe? Yes! Fear? Oh no!

Now he sees the four horsemen of the Apocalypse ride forth. Stars fall from the sky, and earthquakes rock the globe. The mighty of the earth shake in their shoes, but not John! His Friend, Jesus, holds all the keys.

The seven trumpets blare, and now the Devil rules the earth. An angel calls down woes upon the world, and John stands amidst it all unafraid.

A mighty angel holds a little book. John is told to go and take it. "Give it to me," he says to this mighty, majestic lord of another world. And, at once, the book is surrendered into John's outstretched hand (Rev. 10). Bitterness? Yes! Nausea? Yes! Fear? No. What is there to fear? He has been told, "Fear not." He needs to be told it only once. The most horrendous, end-time judgments leave him unmoved. He is immortal till his work is done. And so are we. "Fear not," Jesus says, "I have the keys."

Devotion 97

The Four and Twenty Elders

Revelation 4–5

Amidst scenes of glory that virtually defy description, John contemplates the four and twenty elders. These are the crowned royalties of heaven, angelic beings of high dignity and destiny. They are mentioned seven times in the apocalypse. They seem to be members of a heavenly priesthood, the priesthood that seems to have inspired David to arrange Israel's temple priesthood into twenty-four groups. Almost every time we see these celestial elders, they are off their thrones and down on their faces in worship before God.

We first see them in the company of the cherubim. As the voices of the cherubim awake the echoes of the everlasting hills ("Holy! Holy! Holy!"), these elders respond. Down on their faces they go! And there go their crowns, cast at Jesus' feet. They lift their voices. They say to the Lord of Glory: "Thou art worthy . . . for thou hast created all things" (Rev. 4:11).

Presently the Lamb of Calvary is unveiled in heaven as the only One fit govern the globe. The seven-sealed scroll, the title deed of earth, is given to Him. Down the elders go again as the chanting cherubim proclaim the goodness and glory of God. "Thou art worthy . . . for thou wast slain," is the song the elders sing (Rev. 5:9).

Now all creatures great and small are called upon to pay tribute to the Lamb. From the high halls of heaven they come; from the dark and dreadful dungeons of the damned; up from the deepest depths of the sea; drawn from the utmost bounds of the everlasting hills. Every knee must bow. Every tongue must confess that Jesus Christ is Lord. Down fall the four and twenty elders once again, overwhelmed, thrilled to the core of their being to see the Lamb of God coming into His own at long last (Rev. 5:14).

And, once again, the scene is changed. All hell has been let loose on earth. The Antichrist's gestapo are hunting down all Jews, as well as all

Gentiles converted by the preaching of the 144,000 witnesses. A countless multitude is martyred and received into glory. As these triumphant saints go marching in, the heavenly hosts, the countless angels who surround the elders and the cherubim and the throne of God in glory, fall down on their faces and worship God (Rev. 7:11–17).

Now it is the turn of God's two witnesses (possibly Enoch and Elijah sent back to earth). Long and fierce has been their battle with the Beast in and around Jerusalem, his religious capital. In the end the Beast slays them. God then raises them and raptures them and shakes Jerusalem to its foundations with an earthquake. As these glorious two come marching into glory amidst the cheers of the angelic hosts, and as the angel sounds the seventh and final trumpet, down go the elders again, worshiping on their faces before God (Rev. 11:16–18).

The two witnesses are followed into heaven by the 144,000 witnesses. These fiery evangelists have marched unscathed into every capital of the world, winning converts everywhere. They are given a special rapture into heaven. They sing a new song, standing before the throne of God. The four and twenty elders are enthralled—so enthralled, in fact, that they forget to fall on their faces before God (Rev. 14:1–5)!

And now the time has come for great Babylon, the glittering commercial capital of the Antichrist, the sin showcase of the world, to be judged. Great, sudden, and absolute is its fall. Again the four and twenty elders respond. Down on their faces they go. "Amen! Alleluia," they say (Rev. 19:4).

And that's the last we see of them. Their thrones are now to be vacated. Their place in heaven will be taken by the church-age overcomers, who will come into their own at last and sit enthroned, higher than them all, as coheirs of glory with the Lamb.

Devotion 98

The Name of Mystery

Revelation 19:11–12

Heaven above rings with the shouts of "Hallelujah!" The sound awakes the echoes of the everlasting hills. John says that "much people in heaven" peal out those anthems of praise (Rev. 19:1).

Much people in heaven! "Are there few that be saved?" the disciples once asked (Luke 13:23). It was a good question. The Lord said, "Strait is the gate, and narrow is the way, which leadeth unto life, and few there be that find it" (Matt. 7:14). The kingdom parables (Matt. 13) show similar seeming failure. Great deceptions hinder, if not halt, the onward march of God's activities on earth. But when all God's purposes are done, He will be seen to have the preeminence in all things (Col. 1:18). That surely includes numerical preeminence too.

Perhaps the difference between "the few" referred to in one place and "the much people" referred to in another is to be found somewhere other than in His purposes with the church. For instance, millions upon millions of people will be saved during the Tribulation age (Rev. 7). They will not be in the church, though they will be in the kingdom, and they will be in heaven. And so will all the little children of earth who were victims of infant mortality and never grew to reach the age of accountability. Surely "of such is the kingdom of heaven" (Matt. 19:14).

The hallelujahs in Revelation 19 are heaven's spontaneous response to the sudden and total fall of Babylon and to the marriage supper of the Lamb. This is ushered into history as suddenly, without warning, heaven opens. The warring world looks up to see an invasion taking place from the sky. It is Jesus coming again!

The Holy Spirit now pauses to describe the awesome splendor of the returning Christ and draws our attention particularly to the names of Jesus. Every knee in the universe is soon to bow before the name of Jesus. But for now we are invited to consider some of His other names.

First, there is *the name of mystery*. He has "a name written, that no man knew, but he himself." From time to time in Scripture, during the onward march of things, God has broken into history to *reveal* Himself by many and varied names. But here is a name the purpose of which is not to reveal but *conceal*. This name suggests those deep and hidden depths in the nature, person, and personality of Christ known to Him and His Father alone. One supreme mystery about the person of Christ is that in Him dwells all the fullness of the Godhead *bodily*. "Heaven of heavens cannot contain thee," Solomon said, "much less this house I have builded" (I Kings 8:27). Even less, we might think, could the body of a babe contain Him. But, even as He lay there, cradled in a woman's arms, He was upholding all things by the word of His power. Countless galaxies roared and thundered overhead. It was He who was guiding them on their vast journeys. It is He who stokes the fierce fires that drive them at astounding speeds on orbits too great for us to grasp.

Think of the mystery of it! Deity is clothed in humanity; a Babe lying in a Bethlehem barn in infant attire is the Ancient of Days, arrayed in garments of light.

There He sits at His mother's knee, learning His alphabet, He who is the *Alpha* and the *Omega*, the very alphabet itself.

There He sits by a wayside well. Tired and thirsty, He asks a woman for a drink—the One who engineered Niagara and pours its waters from lake to lake amid the awesome splendor of the falls.

We see Him accept the tribute of a small lad's lunch; He who, had He willed, could have turned stones to bread as simply as He once turned water into wine.

He was truly man in every sense of the word; and He was truly God. Never did He demonstrate His humanity at the expense of His deity. Never did He demonstrate His deity at the expense of His humanity. He always behaved as One who was both God and man.

Think of the mystery of it! And remember He has a name to explain it all. It is a name held high, on a head now crowned with many crowns. But it is "a name written, that no man knew, but he himself" (Rev. 19:12).

Devotion 99

The Name of Ministry

Revelation 19:13

His name is called the Word of God," the Holy Spirit says. That brings us back to more familiar ground, for "the Word of God" is one of John's favorite names for Christ. It is *the name of ministry*. It is the name that mobilizes all that God is to take care of all that we are. The Word! When God wants to accomplish anything, He only has to speak. He speaks, and it is done.

When God decided to act in *creation,* He did so through His word. The factual record of what happened is preserved for us by the Holy Spirit in Genesis 1. Ten times we read: "And God said." Here is God's first set of ten commandments, none of which has ever been broken. They stand in contrast with His second set of ten commandments (Exod. 20), none of which has ever been kept, in spirit and in truth—except by the incarnate Word Himself.

That Word was the active force in creation. "Let there be light," He said, "and there was light" (Gen. 1:3). One word from Him, and an ocean seated itself in the sky, ascending there by the laws of evaporation and descending back down by the laws of precipitation. One word from Him, and life in myriad forms sprang into being and invaded every nook and cranny of the globe. What people call "nature" is merely His handmaid. Behind all of nature is the Word, and "the Word" is just another name for Jesus.

When God decided to act in *revelation,* He did so through His word. He spoke! He wrote things down! Men and women from all walks of life became His instruments. Truth was revealed to them; and, inspired of God, they wrote; and what they said was the inerrant Word of God.

When God decided to act in *redemption,* He did so through His word. The inspired Word did well enough for several thousand years. It told us that a Redeemer was coming, One who could be "near of kin unto us" (Ruth 2:20). Now He has come. John describes Him as "the Word . . . made flesh" (John 1:14). As we clothe our secret thoughts in words and thus make them known, so the Word of God clothed in flesh makes plain to us what God is like. The Son of God became the Son of Man. He became the *incarnate* Word, our near Kinsman, related to us by a common humanity so that He could redeem us as Boaz redeemed Ruth.

When the tabernacle furniture was made, special significance was attached to the ark of the covenant. It was a chest made of acacia wood (incorruptible wood designed by God to survive the hostile environment of the wilderness) and was overlaid with gold. The wood symbolized Christ's sinless humanity, while the gold symbolized His deity. Inside the ark was a pot of manna from the days of the wilderness years (to remind us that God meets our *material* needs); Aaron's rod that budded, a dead stick endued with life anew, bestowed by God (to remind us that God meets all our *spiritual* needs); and an unbroken copy of the Law (to remind us that God meets all our *moral* needs). As that unbrŏken copy of the Law reposed in the sacred ark, even so God's word, unbroken in thought, word, or deed, rested in the heart of God's Son. It was what moved and motivated Him to magnify His Father and to minister to us.

When God finally acts in *retribution,* He will again act through His word. The Holy Spirit tells us of "the sword" that comes out of the mouth of the returning Christ (Rev. 19:15). A sword is used symbolically in Scripture of God's Word, which is living and powerful and sharper than any two-edged sword (Eph. 6:17; Heb. 4:12). Thus He will deal with His foes. One word from Him, and to a lost eternity they go, in a moment, in the twinkling of an eye, swifter than the lightning, surer than the dawn.

"His name is called the Word of God" (Rev. 19:13). It is the name that gets things done, a name that ministers to the glory of God and to the needs of people. That name is written on His blood-drenched robe. One day the Word will be the minister of God's wrath. But for now the Word of God, incarnate in Christ, wears a shining face and bids us to know Him. And to know Him is to know life eternal.

Devotion 100

The Name of Majesty

Revelation 19:14–16

The Holy Spirit has another name to reveal. But first He paints a picture of the Lord. He is treading out the vintage where the grapes of wrath are stored. He has a sharp sword and a rod of iron! The sword tells us how He intends to *retake* the kingdom; the rod of iron tells us how He intends to *rule* the kingdom. Already great Babylon has fallen (Rev. 18). Already earth's armies, East and West, are gathered at Megiddo (Rev. 16:13–16; 19:17–19). Already the birds of prey have been summoned to feast on the multiplied millions of those soon to be dead. And now, descending from the sky, comes the Invader from beyond. He is riding a great white horse (Rev. 19:11). The King of Glory comes!

His vesture catches every eye. Blood red it is, and the battle has not yet begun. And there, on that vesture a name is written: "King of Kings, and Lord of Lords" (Rev. 19:16). Centuries ago Pilate, in bitter irony and wanting to irritate the Jews, wrote a mocking title and hung it over the head of the crucified Christ: "Jesus of Nazareth the King of the Jews" it declared (John 19:19). It drew attention to the *person* they despised, Jesus; and to the *place* they despised, Nazareth; and to the *Prince* they despised. "King" indeed! They would rather have Caesar as king than this meek Messiah, this weak Messiah, dying the death of a slave. They would rather have Barabbas, for at least he had led an insurrection against Rome.

But the title was true just the same. He *was* the King of the Jews. An hour or two in the temple archives would have established that beyond all doubt. The record was available to all. His claim to the throne ran through the line of Joseph (who adopted Him) and through the line of Mary (who bore Him). It ran through David, Bathsheba, and Solomon (Matt. 1:6–16) and through David, Bathsheba, and Nathan (Luke 3:23–31). His claim to the throne was crystal clear. The regal line through Joseph and the natural line through Mary climaxed and culminated in Him. The Lord, raised from the dead, is now the only possible heir to the throne of David. When the expected Jewish delegation arrived, demanding a change in the title now heralding the death of their King on a tree, Pilate sardonically declared: "What I have written I have written" (John 19:22). Thank you, Pilate, for the undeniable fact you proclaimed in that title, and thank you for the unexpected firmness you displayed. Well done! May it be to your credit in the day when the books are opened and the dead judged according to their works, that at least in this you stood firm for the truth.

But here in Revelation 19 it is not the cross that is in view but the *crown*. So, in defiance of all the powers of hell and all the massed millions of earth, one and all drawn to Megiddo for their doom, the full title is displayed: King of Kings and Lord of Lords. The hymn writer well says:

> Sinners in derision crowned Him,
> Mocking thus the Savior's claim;
> Saints and angels crowd around Him,
> Own His title, praise His name.[1]

The armies of the earth, led by their gods and their kings and energized by Satan and his demon hosts, redirect their weapons of mass destruction aimed at each other, and point them at Him. In their abysmal folly they think that they can oppose Him. The second Psalm tells them otherwise. It tells of the terrible laughter of God as He foresees and foretells this very event: "He that sitteth in the heavens shall laugh: the Lord shall have them in derision," the Holy Spirit says (v. 4). That terrible laughter is the last thing they will hear on earth. It will awaken the echoes of the caverns of the damned. And now they know the truth—Jesus of Nazareth, the King of the Jews, is King of Kings and Lord of Lords.

---

1. Thomas Kelly, "Look, Ye Saints! The Sight Is Glorious," 1809.